THE HISTORY OF
PHILOSOPHY

The History of the Humanities and Social Sciences

THE HISTORY OF
PHILOSOPHY

ANNE ROONEY

ROSEN PUBLISHING®

New York

This edition published in 2017 by:
The Rosen Publishing Group, Inc.
29 East 21st Street
New York, NY 10010

Library of Congress Cataloging-in-Publication Data

Rooney, Anne, author.
The history of philosophy / Anne Rooney.
  pages cm.—(The history of the humanities and social sciences)
Includes bibliographical references and index.
ISBN 9781499464009 (library bound)
LCSH: Philosophy—History. | Philosophy—Introductions.
R633 2016
190—dc23
LC record available at http://lccn.loc.gov/2016010410

Manufactured in China

Contents

The examined **LIFE**

"What I really lack is to be clear in my mind what I am to do . . . the thing is to find a truth which is true for me, to find the idea for which I can live and die."

Søren Kierkegaard,
Journals (1836)

Philosophy is just thinking; anyone can do it. And you don't even need to get dressed . . .

The story of philosophy starts in Ancient Greece in the sixth century BCE.

Finding "the truth which is true for me": this is the business of philosophy. It is not a luxury, an abstruse pursuit for those with the time to sit in an ivory tower. It is a tool by which humans can work out how to live, how to endure misfortune, how to think about the world around them and how to relate to others.

It is essentially asking questions – the biggest questions imaginable. Philosophers have asked questions such as: "What is reality?" "Does God exist?" "How can we know if something is true?" "What is virtue?" and "Is what is "right" or "wrong" the same for all people, places and times?"

Does it matter?

You might feel that you can get through life without deciding what reality is, but you will still stumble over philosophy in the questions that crop up for all thinking people in everyday life:

► Do animals have rights?
► Should we allow terminally sick people to die when they choose to?
► If social deprivation pushes someone into crime, should they be punished?
► Does it matter if you avoid paying tax?
► Do people have a right to say things that upset others?

Philosophy provides us with a framework and a toolkit for tackling such questions.

Asking questions

This is a book of questions and some of the attempts made to answer them over the 2,500-year history of Western philosophy. Philosophical questions are not susceptible to a single, correct or "true" answer. Trying to answer them is a task beset with difficulties, not least because philosophers don't agree on what constitutes "truth",

> *"The unexamined life is not worth living."*
> Plato (c.427–347BCE)

8

> *"I doubt, therefore I think, therefore I am."*
>
> René Descartes, *The Discourse on the Method* (1637)

what it means to "know" anything, or even the status of the words we use to express the questions and answers.

In discussing the deep questions that can help us to find "the idea for which I can live and die", we are continuing a dialogue that began with the Ancient Greek philosopher Socrates (470–399BCE) and is unlikely ever to end. As time passes, the world we live in changes and the parameters of the debate shift. Although the world we live in today is very different from the one that Socrates knew, the questions we ask are very similar. We still seek to live a virtuous life, ask whether or not there is a God, and strive to know what is true about the world around us. But advances in scientific knowledge, exposure to very different societies and cultures around the world, and shifting social structures have changed the direction of the debate.

The Ancient Greeks had as firm a conviction that their gods existed as modern Christians, Jews, Muslims and Hindus have that their own gods exist.

The whole can of worms

"There is nothing.
If there were anything, no one would know it.
If anyone did know it, no one could communicate it."

This bleak view of the meaninglessness of existence by the Ancient Greek philosopher Gorgias (c.483–375BCE) makes philosophy look a pretty barren and hopeless endeavour. But it's a starting point, and one that the French philosopher René Descartes was to use two thousand years later when he set out to determine what, if anything, exists and how we can be sure of it. Before we start to look at how philosophers have approached the question of existence, we will pause to think about "being" and "knowing", as the two – though treated separately hereafter – are impossible to separate fully.

Being and knowing

Which do you believe exists:
► Yourself?
► The last person you spoke to?
► The clothes you are wearing?
If you trust the evidence of your senses and your memory, and you trust in the continued existence of something after it has passed out of your sight, you will believe all of these exist.

Even to the casual enquirer, though, the existence of some things is clearly not certain. Here are some things you probably haven't seen. Which, if any of them, do you believe exist:

► Narwhals?
► Atoms?
► Yetis?
► God?
► Fairies?

Most people believe things told to them by sources they consider authoritative. You probably believe I exist, as someone must have written the book and if it was not the "I" that is named on the cover it would be an "I" that is someone else.

Plenty of people have seen narwhals even if you haven't – you can see videos of them on YouTube, and read about their biology. It would take a massive conspiracy for some group to have invented narwhals and then kept the deception going for centuries. Indeed, it's simpler for them to exist than not exist (but that in itself is not evidence of their existence).

> **SPOTLIGHT ON PHILOSOPHERS**
>
> The Greek philosopher Aristotle (384–322BCE) would say we certainly have enough evidence to agree that narwhals exist.
>
> The Anglo-Irish philosopher George Berkeley (1685–1753) would say that even seeing a narwhal yourself doesn't give you irrefutable evidence of their existence.

Most people believe established science gives an accurate account of the world. We haven't seen atoms, but there is plenty of evidence to support their existence. They make sense.

There are signs that might be evidence of yetis, but those signs could have been misinterpreted. No one has indisputably seen yetis. As they would be visible if they existed, this casts doubt on their existence – but it doesn't prove there are no yetis.

What about God? Some people have as firm a conviction that God exists as they

Most revolutions are staged in the name of freedom or equality. But what are they? And are they always the same, from one age to another?

do that they themselves exist. Others deny there is a God at all. Far fewer people believe in fairies – but some do, and more used to. There is no more solid physical evidence for the existence of God than there is for the existence of fairies. Here we have another source of 'evidence' – personal conviction or instinct. Sometimes, a firmly held belief is more convincing to an individual than the evidence of science or reason.

Let's make it a bit harder. Which of these do you believe exist:

► A conversation you had last week?

► Justice?

► The hole in a doughnut?

► A poem you have made up in your head, but not written down or spoken aloud?

Now we are in the realm of things that logically we have to say don't exist and yet we feel they do have some kind of existence. We"ve run up against the problem of what we mean by "exist" – both what is it to "be" and what does the word "exist" mean to us?

A conversation you had last week caused vibrations in the air that have now dissipated. It produced chemical and electrical changes in your brain and the brain of other participants that have now gone. Yet it exists in your memory and that of others present at the time.

"Justice" has no physical existence. It exists purely as a concept in the minds of people and as enshrined in laws. There is no universal agreement about what constitutes justice.

The hole in a ring doughnut is an absence of doughnut rather than part of the doughnut itself, an area of not-doughnut, as it were. But so is your hand an area of not-doughnut. The hole is a hole because we

The dough-not in a doughnut – does it exist?

perceive it as a gap in what should be doughnut-space (let's call it "dough-not"). In fact, the hole is just air but it is defined by what is around it: the context of doughnut makes it a "dough-not".

Think about a poem that you have made up but not written down. It exists in your mind until you forget it or die. Does it have any form of existence (a) now and (b) when you have forgotten it or have died? What if you forgot it, but remembered it later? Would it have existed in between?

SPOTLIGHT ON PHILOSOPHERS

Plato would say that there is an ideal form of justice, which all human attempts at realizing justice strive towards but never attain.

The French writer Michel de Montaigne (1533–92) would say that justice is different in different societies and no one version is better than another in absolute terms.

THE TRUMAN SHOW

The Truman Show (1998) is a film by Peter Weir in which an insurance salesman discovers that his entire life has been a TV show and nothing that he supposed was real actually *is* real. In Truman's thirtieth year, he begins to notice anomalies in his "reality" and investigates before attempting to escape his false world.

So it would seem that some things "exist" as words or concepts (ideas) but not as physical phenomena.

As we can see, being sure of what exists is not quite as straightforward as it looks. Philosophers make it even harder by questioning the foundations of our judgements and beliefs and requiring proof that everything, even the enquiring mind, exists before accepting its claims.

Even when we believe in the existence of something, there is another question to ask – what can we know about it? We can see stars, but are they lights stuck on a celestial sphere as the ancients believed, or balls of gas undergoing nuclear fusion, as modern scientists tell us? How can we know what is true? This is the subject matter of epistemology, the study of knowledge (*see* Chapter 4).

Dealing with it all

Once we"ve accepted that we exist, we have to deal with life. How should we live? Are there any universal moral laws that tell us how to behave? Or do different moral laws apply in different ages, places or circumstances? That is, is morality absolute or relative? Some things seem clear-cut. In most countries it's considered wrong to kill people. But some countries, and certain states in the USA, still have the death penalty and therefore endorse "judicial killing". Many people believe in a "just war" – that we can go to war, inevitably causing some deaths, in support of a "good" cause, such as deposing a tyrant. The victims of war or judicial execution don't generally want to die – and they are rarely given a choice. What about terminally ill people who ask to die? Is it right to kill them? Most countries don't allow this type of killing (euthanasia). How can it be defensible to wage a "just war" in which a child playing in a marketplace is killed accidentally, but not defensible to kill an adult suffering chronic and incurable pain who wants to die? The questions of what is right and wrong, and how we make moral choices, is the subject matter of ethics (*see* Chapter 5).

The issue of how to live can be addressed on an individual and on a societal level. When it extends to issues about social cohesion and law, how a body of people should be governed, it becomes the material of political philosophy (*see* Chapter 6).

Telling the story

Unlike other disciplines, philosophy does not always build on the ideas that have gone before. In physics, we could not have had Einstein

> *"I do not wish to judge how far my efforts coincide with those of other philosophers . . . the reason why I give no sources is that it is a matter of indifference to me whether the thoughts that I have had have been anticipated by someone else."*
>
> Ludwig Wittgenstein,
> *Tractatus Logico-Philosophicus* (1918)

without first having had Newton. In philosophy, anyone can start from scratch. The German philosopher Martin Heidegger, who published his one book in 1927, rejected everything that philosophers before him had said and set out to rebuild philosophy from the ground up. Someone else could do the same tomorrow. In one way this book doesn't offer any answers. Yet in another way it offers too many answers. It presents some of the answers that previous (and present) generations of philosophers have proposed, defended and sometimes overturned. In doing that, it provides a starting point for finding the answers that suit you – that can lead to "the idea for which [you] can live and die".

BRANCHES OF PHILOSOPHY

Metaphysics/Ontology – the study of existence: what exists? What is it to exist?

Epistemology – the study of knowledge: what can we know and how do we know it?

Logic – the study of valid reasoning.

Ethics – the study of right and wrong actions: what should we do?

Politics – the study of force in society: what is allowed?

Aesthetics – the study of art/beauty.

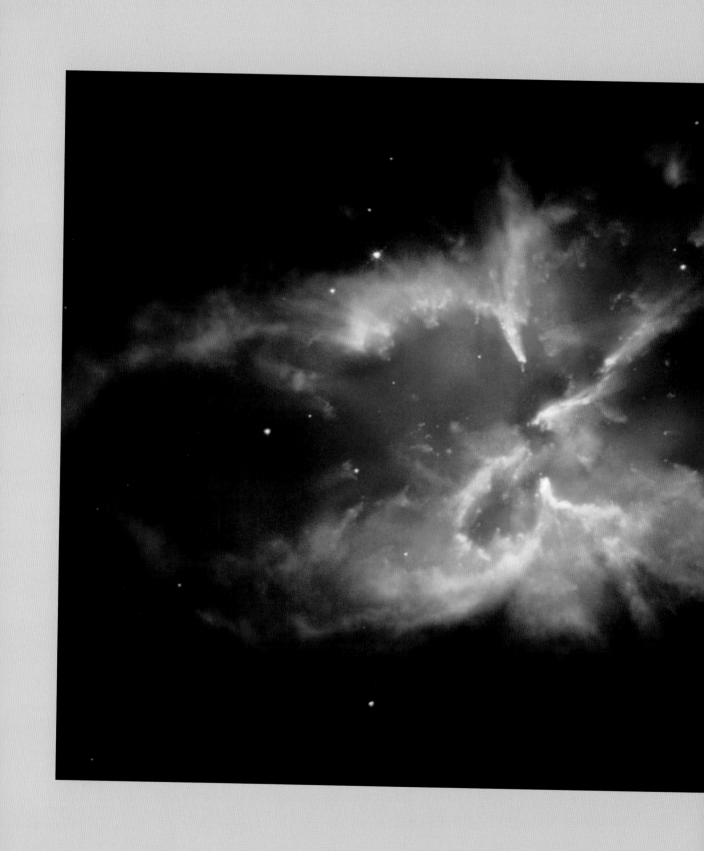

CHAPTER 1

What is
THERE?

"*Nothing exists except atoms and empty space;
everything else is opinion.*"

Attributed to Democritus
(c.460–370BCE)

"*The question is: Why is there any being at all
and not rather Nothing?*"

Martin Heidegger
(1889–1976)

*Does "what there is" include this planetary nebula 10,000 light
years away from Earth?*

The problem of "being"

The nature of "being" has concerned philosophers for at least 2,500 years and probably much longer. Although being and reality are close cousins, not all philosophers agree that they are the same thing. Like so many terms in philosophy, these are open to discussion.

"Being", in the sense of existence, applies not just to humans but also to the physical world around us and the mental, emotional or spiritual world within us.

Reality might – or might not – be something that extends outside ourselves. How reality is constructed (that is, how our minds build a perception of reality) and how or whether it relates to anything real "out there" are questions that get to the heart of being and "what there is". It remains possible that what we call "reality" doesn't exist.

Is there anybody there?

The Ancient Greek philosopher Parmenides (c.510–c.440BCE) was one of the first to tackle the question of what "is". In a fragment of a poem called *On Nature*, Parmenides describes reality as single, undivided, homogenous and unchanging. Presented as a revelation delivered by a goddess, the poem says it is impossible to conceive of or describe something that doesn't exist because even thinking about it gives it some form of existence. This makes sense, but immediately leads us into questions of what we mean by "being".

Working from this idea – that just thinking of something means it "is" – Parmenides presented the first known formal deduction in the history of Western philosophy. It goes like this:

► Thinking of something that "is" implies the existence of something that "is not" – because if we say something "is" a dog that implies it "is not" a cat.

► But we can't say something "is not", as he has already demonstrated.

► Therefore we can't say something specific exists (because saying it "is" something implies it "is not" something else).

► Finally, as we can't discriminate between different things in the world, we can only see them as part of a continuous homogenous reality that has the property of existing.

(You might think this is just a slick trick with words. If we didn't have words for "cat" and "dog", we wouldn't have the problem. But that's getting ahead of ourselves by more than 2,000 years.)

Similarly, things can't change. If we can think of something that will exist in the future, we are giving it some type of existence in our minds now. The same is true of the past: if you remember something that has gone, it exists in your memory. Indeed, everything that can be conceived of exists, even if only in the mind of one individual – and everything is part of one, unchanging, eternal whole.

The good, the bad and the ugly: ideal Forms and the inferior world

Plato (c.427–347BCE) adopted Parmenides" view that reality is unchanging and eternal. But he also recognized that we don't experience the world in that way, and that this disjunction between how the world is and how it seems must be explained.

THERE'S NO SUCH THING AS MONSTERS . . .

Suppose you create a monster in your mind. You know the monster does not "really" exist – it has no external, physical existence in the world – as you"ve just made it up. But in imagining the monster, you give it some form of existence. Clearly existence in the world, in the mind and in language are very different.

We can say a cat exists because cats are familiar to us in the real world. We can say a unicorn exists as they are depicted in literature and art, with established qualities and physical appearance. The monster you have thought up, unnamed, undrawn, unarticulated – does it have any form of existence? If so, what? This question still occupies philosophers in the present day.

Early audiences of the vampire film Nosferatu *(F. W. Murnau, 1922) felt real fear, even though they knew the vampire didn't exist.*

Plato concluded that the world of experience is illusory. There is, he said, a realm of eternal, unchanging "ideal Forms" that act as blueprints for everything that exists in the physical world. What we encounter with our senses are multiple individual instances or copies of the Forms. None of them is a perfect copy. According to Plato, although there are many individual horses, cats and dogs, they are all made in the image of the one universal Form of the "horse", "cat", or "dog". In a famous analogy, he likened the phenomena we experience to the shadows cast on the wall of a cave by firelight flickering behind objects. The ideal, or Form, is the equivalent of an object that casts a shadow; but we only ever see the shadow and never the object itself. We are not even aware that what we see is not "reality". This makes Plato an idealist – one who believes that "reality" is what happens inside the mind or spirit: not the physical world around us, which is only created by our minds struggling to comprehend reality.

As Plato extended the theory of Forms to everything, it follows that all individuals are made in the image of the universal Form of the human. This last was easy for Christian thinkers to work with later, as it fits in with the Christian doctrine that all humans are made in the image of God. It helped one of the founders of the early Christian church, St Augustine of Hippo (CE354–430),

THE ALLEGORY OF THE CAVE

In his famous dialogue *The Republic* (c.380BCE), Plato describes a group of people who have spent their whole lives chained up inside a cave. All they can see are shadows cast on a wall by the light of a fire as people move around just out of view carrying objects, such as carved figures of animals. The chained-up people come up with ideas about the nature of reality, but all their ideas are based on the shadows they see and what they can deduce from them. If one person were to free himself and see the world as it truly is, he would at first be blinded by the light and confused by what he saw, and find it hard to adapt. If he then returned to the cave, he would find it difficult to persuade the others that what they see is not reality. They would resist his lessons, and even condemn him as mad. The person who escapes is, Plato said, like the philosopher, who attempts to see beyond the shadows to the Forms – the true reality that lies behind what we see.

to accommodate Plato's metaphysics into a Christian schema and secure the Ancient Greek philosopher's enduring influence over European philosophy.

Plato didn't restrict his theory to physical objects. He also thought there were ideal Forms of concepts such as beauty, justice and truth, and even of mathematical ideas such as number and class. As recently as the 20th century, Gottlob Frege (1848–1925) and Kurt Gödel (1906–78) endorsed this aspect of Plato's thoughts, considering numbers to have absolute reality as Forms.

Plato maintained that there was a separate realm, apart from the observable physical universe, where these Forms lurked. Where might that be? One possibility is that they might be outside time and space. Later, neoplatonists, such as Plotinus and St Augustine, claimed that these Forms reside in the mind of God.

The problem of universals – or "is there such a thing as red?"

The English friar and philosopher William of Ockham, who died in 1347, took a view that was directly opposite to that of Plato. He stated that universals do not exist outside human understanding, and that terms such as "redness", or even "man" are just ways of collecting together many individual objects for psychological simplicity. In reality there are only individuals, and all types of categorization are imposed and artificial.

In modern terminology, this makes Ockham a *nominalist* – someone for whom the only existence of universals is as a name for something. Plato, on the other hand, was a *realist* – someone who believes universals have existence.

PHILOSOPHERSPEAK: NOMINALISM

Nominalism states that non-physical concepts such as "justice", "green" or "twelve" have no existence beyond the words that name them. It's possible to have a severe case of nominalism, or only slight nominalism.

Predicate nominalists say that green things are green only because the predicate green is applied to all of them. (A *predicate* is a word describing a property of a subject.) "Green" has no existence outside the word, and there is nothing other than use of the word that unites green things. This leaves unanswered how we decide to apply the word "green" to something, but allows that two people might not experience the same thing when they look at something "green".

Resemblance nominalists say that things are called "green" if they sufficiently resemble an exemplar (Plato's ideal Form) of "green" and resemble that more than they resemble another, competing, exemplar, such as "purple".

The Ancient Greek philosopher Aristotle was also a realist, but of a different flavour. Aristotle believed universals only had existence if they were "instantiated" (that is, if there were real, tangible instances of them), whereas Plato believed universals have absolute existence, independently of their instantiation. Suppose all human life were extinguished. For Plato, universals such as childhood, cruelty and chastity would still exist, but for Aristotle they would not exist, as they could not be instantiated – there would no longer be real, tangible examples to draw on.

All, nothing or something?

Plato's pupil Aristotle picked the common-sense position that is the default for most people in their everyday dealings with the world. He argued that reality exists independently of the human mind, and makes up the world of physical objects and phenomena that we find around us. For Aristotle, matter exists and it is given "substantial form" by some kind of organizing principle. It is the organizing principle that gives different types of matter their distinctive properties and "potentialities" or powers. So the physical material that makes up everything from tables to giraffes is the same, while the "substantial form" gives some things "table-ness" and other things "giraffe-ness".

To summarize, there are two opposing positions in relation to reality:

Aristotle, who studied under Plato, eventually disagreed with many of his tutor's ideas.

> **PHILOSOPHERSPEAK: NEOPLATONISM**
> Neoplatonism is a philosophy that follows the work of Plato but extends or adapts it, focusing on spiritual and mystical aspects. It is generally considered to have started with the work of Plotinus (c.CE204–270).

Idealism (Plato): Everything we experience in the world and think of as reality is an illusion created by our imperfect senses; the realm of ideal Forms is not directly accessible to us.

Realism (Aristotle): The external world exists independently of humans being present to experience it. Universals exist only when they are instantiated – so if all red things vanished, red itself would no longer exist.

These two basic positions have given rise to different variants and emphases since the time of the Ancient Greeks. Between the polar extremes of idealism and realism, there is a dualist position that allows both matter and something insubstantial to exist. Actually, dualism is more than one position – there are plenty of variants. But in essence it sees a distinction between the physical and the non-physical (particularly but not exclusively in terms of the human), then struggles to build bridges between them. The question that most troubles dualists is, how can the physical interact with the non-physical, and vice versa? Yet everyday common sense tells us that it does. If you fall down and break a leg, it causes physical damage and pain. It also makes you miserable, frustrated, angry – mental states apparently caused by a physical state or event. Dualism is covered in more detail in Chapter 3.

MULTIPLE REALITIES

The American philosopher David Kellogg-Lewis (1941–2001) went beyond the concept of "all or nothing" and opted for an "even more than all" position. Adapting the "many worlds" theory proposed by physicist Hugh Everett, he claimed that all possible worlds exist and are real, though spatially and temporally separate (so you can't slip into a parallel world if things go wrong for you here). He believed that all these worlds have equivalent concrete reality. Kellogg considered that an innate understanding of this state of affairs is evident in us ever considering statements such as the following to be true: "If I had eaten that very old sandwich, I would have been sick." (In philosophical terms, this statement is a "counterfactual conditional".) The statement supposes that there is another world in which "I" did eat the sandwich and was sick.

In the "many worlds" theory, there are worlds in which Germany won the Second World War, worlds in which the dinosaurs were not wiped out, and worlds in which you were never born.

But really, about *being*

With Aristotle, philosophers stopped looking at "being" *per se*, and began considering how we can *know* what exists. But then, in 1927, the German philosopher Martin Heidegger (1889–1976) suggested that Western philosophy had been concentrating on the wrong kind of questions since the age of Plato. While Plato's metaphysics and Aristotle's epistemology had centerd on what exists, what we can know about what exists, and what properties those "things" have, Heidegger said we need to take a step back and to ask first what we mean by "existence" or "being". As he focused on the question "What is being?" he realized that we also have to ask why there is something rather than nothing. If we were designing philosophy from the ground up, these would be the first questions to ask. Heidegger decided to overturn the philosophical legacy of the preceding 2,500 years and start afresh.

Aristotle talked of "being as such", meaning the essence of being without regard to any specific type of being (neither the "being" that is living – a person or a dog, say – nor the being that is inanimate existence – a table or a pen). Heidegger would start from there.

> **PHILOSOPHERSPEAK: METAPHYSICS**
> Metaphysics means "beyond physics". This branch of philosophy deals with questions of being, reality and existence. It is what Aristotle called "first philosophy".

The being in the world

Heidegger used the term *Dasein* – "being there" – for the being that exists. He rejected the idea that there is an external world separate from a conscious observer (the position of Cartesian dualism). Instead, he developed a *phenomenological* view, in which our understanding of things is always in relation to ourselves. For example, if you put on a jumper, it is because the jumper will keep you warm, or you think it will look good on you. It is not because the jumper is made of twisted yarn and is a few millimeters thick – that is of no interest or relevance to you. This applies to knowledge, too. We might read a book about politics because it interests us, or because understanding politics helps us make sense of what we see happening around us. We see it in terms of a tool, or satisfying a need.

Heidegger saw the *Dasein* (principally the human "being") as completely immersed in and part of the world that defines it. No separation between consciousness and environment is possible.

Martin Heidegger is considered one of the greatest philosophers of the 20th century.

"Being *there*" means that "there" – our context – is the defining aspect of "being". We are not shut off from the world in an enclosed mind – which Heidegger calls the "cabinet of consciousness". For him, the distinction between "out there" (in the world and "inside" (our minds) was invalid.

There is, though, a difference between the "being" of an animate creature and an inanimate object. A chair or a ship has static being, but humans are aware of passing, finite time – a moment in time is part of the "there" we inhabit. Our consciousness of our own being is defined by time and by the knowledge that we will die. This aspect of Heidegger's thinking was taken up by existentialists such as Jean-Paul Sartre (1905–80) and Albert Camus (1913–60).

Why is there?

Once we have asked "what is there?" then, unless the answer is "nothing", we are bound to ask "why is there?" (whatever "there" is), and "why am I?"

We can't know when humans first started to ask questions such as "why do I exist?" or "what makes me alive?" It was probably long before written culture

> "The perception of what is known does not take place as a return with one's booty to the "cabinet" of consciousness after one has gone out and grasped it. Rather, in perceiving, preserving and retaining, the Da-sein *that knows remains outside as* Da-sein. *In "mere" knowledge about a context of the being of beings . . . in "solely" thinking about it, I am no less outside in the world together with beings than I am when I* originally *grasp them. Even forgetting something, when every relation of being to what was previously known seems to be extinguished, must be understood as a modification of primordial being-in, and this holds true for every deception and every error."*
>
> Martin Heidegger,
> *Being and Time* (1927)

began. The earliest answers to those questions that we know of are religious. Perhaps once people began to make things from clay or wood or bone, the inevitable next step was to posit a superhuman entity to try to explain how they themselves came to be "made". An individual who feels the wonder of existence, who is aware of inspiration, love, hate, hope and despair – and who believes that there is a spirit animating himself or herself – might well come to believe that this spirit is somehow the cause and purpose of existence.

FIRST MISTAKES

The Greek philosopher Andronicus of Rhodes collected Aristotle's works around 60BCE. It's thought that he put the writings on "first philosophy" straight after Aristotle's *Physics*, and therefore called them τὰ μετὰ τὰ φυσικὰ βιβλία (*ta meta ta physika biblia*) or "the books that come after the [books on] physics" This was later confusingly shortened to "*meta physika*" or "beyond physics", giving us the term "metaphysics".

First movers

The origin and cause of all things is often called the "first mover" or "prime mover". For the religious, the first mover is a god. That can put a stop to further questions in a religion that doesn't allow its believers to question the origins or purposes of their god. The Greeks had legends to explain the existence of their gods, but still had to come back to a first mover of some type. In some versions, the job was given to Chronos (time), and Chaos (the void), with the primeval gods coming from one or both of these entities. The idea that the universe formed out of time and space or chaos is remarkably close to modern cosmological theory.

A "why" without gods

The first person known to have looked for a non-mystical explanation for the existence of things is the philosopher Thales (c.624–c.546BCE), who was born in the Ancient Greek port of Miletus (now in Turkey). He is considered the father of western philosophy. If Thales wrote anything, none of it survives: we know of his life and ideas only through reports made by Aristotle and other Ancient Greek writers such as the historians Herodotus (484–425BCE) and Plutarch (c.CE46–120), and particularly the 3rd century BCE biographer Diogenes Laertius. But it seems from them that Thales" approach was ground-breaking. In an age when society explained the nature

This French cave painting, 31,000 years old, is part of a depiction of 13 different species of animals and is one of the oldest known examples of humans making images of animate beings.

The easiest way to explain why anything exists is by means of a divine creator. But that just pushes the question backwards: why does the creator exist?

of the world through stories about the wills and whims of anthropomorphic gods, Thales sought to find a common, underlying principle to explain the world around him.

Aristotle reports that Thales thought the Earth floated on water, just as a log or a ship floats on the sea. So instead of earthquakes being caused by angry gods, Thales proposed that the land was rocked by waves from underneath – a view remarkably close in some ways to modern plate tectonics in which earthquakes are explained by the movement of the Earth's plates on a bed of fluid magma. Well, he was wrong about the water, but the principle – that the physical processes of the world can be ascribed to natural, not supernatural, causes – laid the foundations of modern science.

Bean counter

Thales died around 546BCE, by which time the Ancient Greek philosopher and mathematician Pythagoras (*c.*570–495BCE) was around 25 years old. He, too, sought an explicable basis for the natural world and he found it in numbers, much as modern-day scientists attempt to explain the forces of the universe in terms of mathematical rules. Pythagoras mingled his math with a fair dose of mysticism, and the school he founded was distinctly cultish. His followers were not allowed to touch a white cockerel, look into a mirror set beside a light, or eat beans (*see* panel opposite).

Pythagoras also had a strong belief in the transmigration of souls – the idea that the soul survived death and entered another living creature, which might be human or animal. Vegetarianism was the inevitable outcome of this belief, as any potential meaty meal could house the soul of a former (or future) friend or relative.

Metaphysics and physics

Thales and Pythagoras set humankind on the path to what we now call science (from the Latin "*scienta*", knowledge). The scientific way of thinking is a branch of philosophy. Indeed, until the late 19th century, scientific endeavour was called "natural philosophy". The subject of natural philosophy emerged alongside scientific thinking: something

that aims to discover what is demonstrably true. The first professorial chair in Natural Philosophy was at the University of Padua, in 1577. When Pythagoras concluded that the universe ran according to laws that are independent of human knowledge of them, he did not have the resources to prove it – it was a theory and a belief, as much as the existence of the Greek gods was a theory and a belief. When Newton concluded the same thing, he was able to use mathematics and scientific instruments to demonstrate that these rules do, indeed, appear to exist. The movements of the planets follow certain rules. The movement of a falling body, or a cannonball shot from a cannon, also follows rules.

Not quite there

Science has a non-mystical explanation for how the universe and life on Earth came about. But that still doesn't answer the basic questions: Where did the "what/ever" of the Big Bang come from? Why did it come about? How and why did life emerge from inanimate chemicals? Whether we personally prefer the religious or scientific explanation for the origins of life and the universe, both stumble over the question: where did the "first mover" (God/material of the Big Bang) come from? And why? Religion says "don't ask, it's a mystery, it's beyond understanding"; science says "we don't know yet". Both sometimes say "it was always there" or that "time and space/God have no start and no end". For this reason, religion and science are not necessarily mutually exclusive.

DON'T BE MEAN TO THE BEAN!

Pythagoras held beans to be sacred. He banned the eating of meat and of beans by his followers. Several reasons for this have been suggested, including that "they are like genitals" (testicles), or that "they are like the gates of Hades, [the stems] alone [of all plants] being without joints" (both from Aristotle). This last point possibly meant that the hollow stem of a bean plant was considered the conduit for souls on their way to being transmigrated. It's supported by another odd belief, that "eating beans is the same as eating the heads of one's parents". This would explain Pythagoras's injunction to protect both beans and bean plants from animals, and the legend that he allowed his enemies to kill him rather than run away through a bean field, which would damage the beans.

In this 17th century painting by Peter Paul Rubens, Pythagoras (seated, with legs crossed) advocates vegetarianism to his followers.

CHAPTER 2

Is there a
GOD?

"If I saw no signs of a divinity, I would fix myself in denial. If I saw everywhere the marks of a Creator, I would repose peacefully in faith. But seeing too much to deny Him, and too little to assure me, I am in a pitiful state, and I would wish a hundred times that if a God sustains nature it would reveal Him without ambiguity."

Blaise Pascal,
Pensées (1669)

"The interest I have to believe a thing is no proof that such a thing exists."

Voltaire,
Remarks on the Thoughts of Pascal XI

Is the universe ordered and controlled by a divine being?

One answer commonly given to the question "why is there?" is "God." It's also an aspect of "what is there?" – does the what/ever there is include a God? And if so, what is that God like?

Does God exist?

There are several approaches to God and to proof of his existence:

► The complexity of the world or the universe and all that is in it indicates a designer, since it is inconceivable that such a system would come about by chance (the cosmological argument).

► Everything has to be caused by something, so there must be a first cause, and that is what we shall call God (the teleological argument).

► Because we can imagine a God, there must be one (the ontological argument).

► Faith – inner, personal conviction – tells us there is a God so there must be.

None of these "proofs" is satisfactory in philosophical terms, and there are several problems with the notion of "God" that philosophers have attempted to answer – again, not entirely satisfactorily. For those who believe in God, the paucity of the arguments for God's existence is no reason for giving up on him. Indeed, the very nature of faith is that it stands outside reason, so if God *does* exist, his existence need not be susceptible to proof.

PHILOSOPHERSPEAK: THEISM

Theism is the belief in a single god who is omnipotent (all powerful), omniscient (all knowing) and benevolent. Christianity, Judaism and Islam are all theistic religions.

I think, therefore he is

For many philosophers throughout history, belief in God was the default position – they lived in societies in which the existence of God was not generally doubted, and in some cases even to question it was a crime. St Anselm (1033–1109), who was archbishop of Canterbury from 1093, was the first to try to prove the existence of God by reason.

By Anselm's time, the works of Plato and Aristotle had been rediscovered and the Christian philosophers, called scholastics, were attempting to integrate them into their theology.

It is said that Anselm's students, after studying the Greek philosophers, wanted to hear a rational justification for the existence of God. Aristotle and Plato had cited the complexity of the world as evidence of the existence of their gods. Anselm's reply – the ontological argument for the existence of God – has become one of the most debated issues in philosophy:

Suppose that by the term "God" we mean the greatest, most powerful thing that we can think of. The existence of God would then seem to follow necessarily from the definition because . . .

► A God imagined that does not exist is not as great as one imagined that does exist.

► It would be a contradiction to suppose that God is both the greatest thing that can be thought of and also does not exist.

► Since we can clearly think of God and suppose he exists, then he must exist.

There's obviously something wrong with this argument.

Anselm's first critic was a contemporary, the Benedictine monk Gaunilo of Marmoutiers. He argued that if Anselm's reasoning were correct, we could imagine a lost island that was the most perfect island there could ever be. Since by definition it is the most perfect, it must exist as otherwise it would be less than perfect. As Anselm's reasoning could lead to the existence of all sorts of imaginary objects, it must be

---

PHILOSOPHERSPEAK: SCHOLASTICISM

The scholastics were Christian philosophers working in the medieval universities (*c.*1100–1500). Their method, *scholasticism*, proceeds through the dialectic approach – asking a question, proposing an answer, refuting that answer, and so on, to arrive at a conclusion. The scholastics" aim was to bring together two broad sources of authority: Christian (the Bible and the writings of the Church Fathers) and classical (principally Aristotle and Plato, the latter filtered through the neoplatonists).

---

at fault. In response, Anselm said that perfection only applies to God, so the ontological argument can't be used to prove the existence of imaginary islands or anything else other than God.

Ongoing debate

Many philosophers agree that the problem with Anselm's argument revolves around making the meaning of a word or concept the basis on which we decide whether something exists, an objection raised by Thomas Aquinas (1225–74). But philosophers and logicians still debate exactly which logical error is involved. For philosophy, the obvious fact that something is nonsensical isn't good enough – it must be possible to prove that it's nonsense if it is to be dismissed.

The French philosopher and mathematician René Descartes (1596–1650) is often called the father of modern

St Anselm of Canterbury was a renowned teacher, and is considered the father of scholasticism.

PHILOSOPHERSPEAK: ONTOLOGY

Ontology is the study of existence and of what exists.

---

philosophy. He had his own version of the ontological argument that was extremely simple – so simple, in fact, that it is more a self-evident axiom. He says that as the essence of a supreme being includes that it exists, God must exist. The argument is built on other ideas, including that the idea of God is native to the mind.

The German philosopher Immanuel Kant (1724–1804) pointed out that as essence does not presuppose existence, the essence of a supreme being can be what it likes – it doesn't mean the supreme being has to exist. In addition, the argument presupposes that existence is an attribute of perfection – perhaps it is not. Even so, the ontological argument has sufficient appeal that philosophers keep returning to it.

> "Nor do I seek to understand that I may believe, but I believe that I may understand. For this, too, I believe, that, unless I first believe, I shall not understand."
>
> St Anselm of Canterbury,
> *Discourse (Proslogion)* (1077–8)

In the 1960s, the American philosopher Norman Malcolm (1911–90) revived a variant of the argument that avoids previous objections. He redefined God as an "absolutely unlimited being" and then proceeded as follows:

► Any being whose existence depended on something else, or which could be prevented from existing by something else, would be limited and so not God.

► For any proposed being, existence can be possible (but not necessary), necessary, or impossible.

► If its existence is possible but not necessary, the being exists in some possible worlds but not in others. Its non-existence in the others suggests something, or the lack of something, prevents it existing, so it is not an unlimited being.

► If something that is "possible but not necessary" is not an unlimited being, God's existence can't be "possible but not necessary".

► God is therefore either impossible or necessarily exists.

The task remains to prove that God is not impossible.

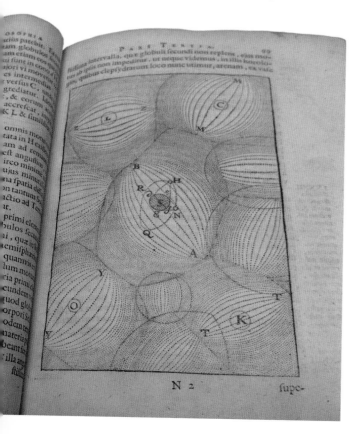

René Descartes" Principia Philosophiae; *this copy was printed in 1656.*

on the way towards a proof. He developed the cosmological argument from Aristotle's contention that there must be a "first mover" that put everything else in motion.

The first way – proving the existence of God through the existence of change:

► Some things in the world are in the process of change.

► Change must be caused by something else, as a thing can't spontaneously change of its own accord.

► This cause must itself by initiated by something.

► We must continue this chain of cause and effect *ad infinitum* unless we posit a "first mover". That first mover is God.

Immanuel Kant maintained that what a thing is essentially "like" is not connected to whether it exists.

Ground zero

Another critic of Anselm's ontological argument was St Thomas Aquinas. He was uncomfortable with its requirement that mere humans have to be able to conceive of God, who is transcendent and so inconceivable. Indeed, his criticism of the ontological argument was so thorough that Anselm's position completely lost credibility for several centuries, resurfacing with Descartes, only to be rebuffed again.

Aquinas presented perhaps the most lucid and concise logical arguments for the existence of God. His "Five Ways", or five steps to proving God exists, appear in his *Summa Theologica* (1266–73). He did not consider these absolute proofs, but steps

St Thomas Aquinas became the favoured philosopher of the Catholic church.

The second way is similar to the first. It is based on the assumption that a thing can't cause itself but must have an external cause. It ends, rather paradoxically, by concluding that there must be one thing that causes itself and that thing is God. Several philosophers have complained that Aquinas" thinking is confused, as the proposition he seeks to prove is the very proposition that he denies in the course of the argument.

The third way relies on change:

► We notice in the world that things come into being and also cease to exist.
► Clearly, not everything can be transient, or there would have been a time when nothing existed, and nothing could be generated from that – something cannot come from nothing.
► Something must always have existed, and that something is what we call God.

This recalls the argument by the Ancient Greek philosopher Parmenides that nothing can come out of nothing, so something (being) must have always existed. These first three ways are variations of the cosmological argument.

The fourth way is a version of Anselm's ontological argument:

► Things can exhibit varying degrees of a quality, such as being more or less hot or good.
► Varying degrees of a quality are caused by something that itself exhibits the perfect

amount of a quality – so the sun, which is the hottest thing, bestows heat on other things.
► For some things to exhibit goodness, there must be a thing that is entirely "good" and that thing is God.

The fifth way draws on Aristotle's notion of *telos*, or purpose, and is a teleological argument:

► All things aim towards some ultimate goal or end.
► Some mind must direct or intend that purpose; it is God that lies behind it.

THOMAS AQUINAS (1225–74)

Thomas Aquinas was born in Sicily, educated at the universities of Naples and Cologne, and lectured at Paris and Naples. He was canonized in 1323 by Pope John XII.

Much of Aquinas" work is derived from Aristotle and consists of trying to reconcile Aristotle's works with Christian teaching (a reconciliation that Augustine achieved for Plato's works). Aquinas also clarified and extended Aristotle's ideas. His huge *Summa Theologica*, or *Summary of Theology*, contains the "Five Ways" – perhaps the clearest attempt ever to prove the existence of God through logical argument. The first part of the *Summa* discusses God, creation and human nature; the second part deals with morality; and the third part begins to deal with Christ and the sacraments. Aquinas never finished the third part, giving up one day after experiencing a mystical vision compared to which, he said, all he had written seemed like straw.

"If the hand does not move the stick, the stick will not move anything else."

Thomas Aquinas,
Summa Theologica (1266–73)

NOT THE FIRST . . .

Aquinas was not the first post-classical proponent of the first-cause theory. The Muslim philosopher Avicenna, or Ibn Sīnā (*c.*CE980–1037), attempted to integrate elements of Aristotle's and Plato's philosophy with his religious belief in God as the Creator. The commentaries of Avicenna and contemporary Muslim scholars were translated into Latin and entered Europe through Spain, greatly influencing the work of Aquinas and the scholastics. Avicenna's argument to prove the existence of God is remarkably similar to that of Aquinas:

► Things come in and out of existence, so existence is not itself an essential property.

► If something comes into existence, there must be a cause for that happening.

► There can't be an infinite chain of caused events without a first cause setting them off.

► This first cause is self-existent and is, of course, God.

Although modern philosophers have almost all rejected Aquinas" Five Ways, the Catholic Church still holds to versions of them.

By the end of the 13th century, then, cosmological, teleological and ontological arguments for the existence of God had been put forward. What came after were largely refinements of these arguments, attempts to bolster them, or critical assaults on them. A few other claims – such as that miracles prove divinity – don't really constitute arguments for the existence of God. (If we accept that a miracle has occurred, that only really demonstrates the veracity of miracles, not of God.)

Damned if you don't: Pascal's wager

Whether or not God exists is not a purely philosophical question. For anyone who believes – or might believe – in a God who takes an interest in humans and doles out rewards and punishments, the existence or non-existence of God is usually tied up with the possibility of an afterlife, and

---

PHILOSOPHERSPEAK: TELEOLOGICAL

A **teleological** argument is one that relates to purpose, intention or aims.

---

hence of eternal damnation or salvation. That focuses the mind more than simple intellectual curiosity.

The French rationalist Blaise Pascal (1623–62) generally supported a rigorously scientific approach to knowledge, but held that different rules apply when we talk about God. In matters beyond the reach of reason, Pascal said that all we can do is rely on the authority of sacred texts. In fact, he was a deeply religious man, and in the last years of his life spent much of his time putting together his *Thoughts* (*Pensées*). This work, a collection of jottings rather than a single, narrative argument, is a form of *apologia* for Christianity. In it he deals with the limitations of reason and the lack of absolute certainty.

The most influential point in *Pensées* is Pascal's "wager" about the existence of God. It is not really an argument for the existence of God, but in favour of belief in God as a rational position:

Either God exists or he does not. We can't discover which is true from reason, but we must choose either to believe or not believe. We must make a wager.

▶ If God does not exist, we lose nothing by believing that he does – death brings annihilation whether we believe or not.

▶ But if he does exist, then we stand to gain everything (salvation) by believing that he does, and to lose everything (damnation) by thinking that he doesn't.

PHILOSOPHERSPEAK: APOLOGIA

An *apologia*, or apology, is a reasoned argument in defence of a position.

▶ Therefore, it is sensible to act as though he does exist: "If you gain, you gain all; if you lose, you lose nothing."

One obvious objection to Pascal's wager, made around a hundred years later by the French philosopher Denis Diderot (1713–84), is that there are actually many wagers to be made. Pascal dealt only with the God of Catholic Christianity, but there are and have been many different gods and belief systems throughout history and we need to choose one of them. Pascal might make his wager, live according to the dictates of the Catholic church, die and be damned because he should have been following Krishna, or Thor, or Zeus.

Choosing the better way

The American psychologist and philosopher William James (1842–1910), the brother of the novelist Henry James, proposed another pragmatic approach to belief. He saw life as full of choices, some of which were "forced", by which he meant an answer must be given as sitting on the fence is not an option. He saw belief in God as a forced choice – if you don't choose to believe you have chosen the other option, non-belief.

Some choices were also "momentous" – they made a huge difference to life. The decision to believe in God was one he regarded as momentous, arguing that choosing to believe gave a person a moral and psychological structure, enriched their life and gave them purpose. He saw nothing to be gained by non-belief, and so the sensible person would always choose to believe. The reasoning is even shakier than that of Pascal, as not only does it not promote one religion over another, but it

> *"I should be much more afraid of being mistaken and then finding out that Christianity is true than of being mistaken in believing it to be true."*
> Blaise Pascal, *Pensées* (1669)

The Maori believe the god Tāne separated the sky and earth, put the stars in the sky and, in some versions, created the first humans. If this is the true religion, a lot of us are in trouble.

doesn't promote religion of any kind over another scheme that might give a person's life focus and purpose.

No need of proof

For some philosophers, the whole concept of proving the existence of God has been either anathema or irrelevant. One such was the Dutch Christian humanist Desiderius Erasmus (1466–1536). Erasmus was particularly impatient with the hypocrisy and worldliness of the Catholic church, and had no truck with the scholastics and their dealings with Plato and Aristotle. Rather, he aligned himself with Augustine and his simple avowals of faith. For Erasmus, belief in God was not a matter of reason but of pure faith.

His book *In Praise of Folly* (1509) satirizes and criticizes the Church, attacking the monastic orders for their apparent belief that living a good religious life consisted in "the precise number of knots to the tying on their sandals". Instead, he argues, true religion is "worship from the heart" and does not need the church as intermediary. Religion is a form of folly in that it is simple, direct and not snarled up in complex doctrine. It must be based on pure, thorough humanism – confidence in the human spirit to recognize and worship God.

Erasmus was as much concerned with the institution of the Church as with proving the existence of God, but the idea that the spirit naturally comprehends and yearns towards God became a powerful non-rational argument for God's existence.

HOW MANY ANGELS CAN DANCE ON THE POINT OF A NEEDLE?

It's difficult to exaggerate the levels of intricacy and ingenuity in scholastic and theological arguments. The suggestion that philosophers debated how many angels could dance on the point of a needle, or the head of a pin, does not seem to be borne out by the surviving texts, though. The earliest reference to this supposed question is in the mid-17th century:

"And Schibler with others, maketh the difference of extension to be this, that Angels can contract their whole substance into one part of space, and therefore have not *partes extra partes*. Whereupon it is that the Schoolmen have questioned how many Angels may fit upon the point of a Needle?"

Richard Baxter, *The Reasons of the Christian Religion* (1667).

It's possible that the question was a debating exercise, to train young scholars in the art of debate, or that it existed only in parodic form to mock the nicety or absurdity of the questions debated.

Although there was a lot of serious debate about angels and their nature, their dancing habits rarely feature.

"It will be pretty to hear their pleas before the great tribunal: one will brag how he mortified his carnal appetite by feeding only upon fish: another will urge that he spent most of his time on earth in the divine exercise of singing psalms . . . but Christ will interrupt: "Woe unto you, scribes and Pharisees, I left you but one precept, of loving one another, which I do not hear anyone plead that he has faithfully discharged.""

Desiderius Erasmus, *In Praise of Folly* (1509)

Faith and reason

While Erasmus objected to the Church's way of dealing with religion, he was not denying the central beliefs of Christianity – the literal existence of God, the physical incarnation of Christ, and so on. A move away from the precise formulation of the divine presented by religious doctrine and authority marked the Age of Enlightenment, which began soon after Erasmus" death.

The French philosopher François-Marie Arouet (1694–1778), who is better known by his pen name "Voltaire", was among those to take a more liberal view of God. He did not feel that belief in any particular brand of religion was necessary for an understanding of the divine. Neither, interestingly, did he feel that blind faith was necessary. He was able to reconcile his belief in the divine with his trust that everything in both the physical and moral/spiritual spheres is governed by explicable, if not yet discovered, laws:

"What is faith? Is it to believe that which is evident? No. It is perfectly evident to my mind that there exists a necessary, eternal, supreme, and intelligent being. This is no matter of faith, but of reason."

The Jewish-Dutch philosopher Baruch Spinoza (1632–77) was also keen to affirm the existence of a divinity (and was a fan of the ontological argument for that purpose) but disinclined to follow any particular body of religious teaching. He is often considered to be the original pantheist, though this simplifies his position somewhat. Spinoza believed that all there is forms one whole, and that the whole is a supreme divine being. This means that while the natural world *is* God, it's not all that God is. Rather, it's a subset of God. His concept of God was the opposite of Judeo-Christian belief in that Spinoza's God had no anthropomorphic qualities – no personality, no incarnation, no will nor intentions, no consciousness. Everything that happens follows necessarily from

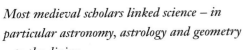

Most medieval scholars linked science – in particular astronomy, astrology and geometry – to the divine.

PHILOSOPHERSPEAK: PANTHEISM

Pantheism is the belief that God is manifest in the whole of the natural universe and is inseparable from it. God is not anthropomorphized and has no will, purpose or consciousness

---

trappings – attending church, reciting scripture and so on – have nothing to do with the religious life, which must involve a personal and direct confrontation with the divine.

the nature, rather than the will, of God, following immutable laws that are not of his making. To all intents and purposes, this made Spinoza an atheist in 17th-century terms and he was expelled from the Jewish community by *cherem* (excommunication and curse) in 1656 for his "monstrous deeds" and "abominable heresies".

While Voltaire found belief in God to be an act of reason, Søren Kierkegaard (1813–55) held religion to be a matter of passion not reason, by necessity. Reason can only undermine faith, he claimed, and never justify it. Rationalistic proofs of God's existence, such as those given by Anselm or Aquinas, have nothing at all to do with a belief in God. An authentic belief acquires its force from within, as a "leap of faith", without reason reassuring us that what we are doing is the right thing. If God's existence were susceptible to rational reflection, there would be no need of faith and it would be meaningless.

Despite this fiercely religious spirit, Kierkegaard attacked the organized Church, which he considered to be the very antithesis of Christianity. He felt that the

God is dead – or was never there

Of course, one reason it might be difficult to prove the existence of God is that he doesn't exist. This is a position that has been difficult for philosophers to take in many times and places. In a thoroughly engodded society (that is, one in which belief in God is universal), a philosopher who stands up to say "there is no God" might at best be ridiculed and at worst be executed. But that option became available around the 18th century, once the Age of Reason was well underway and the stranglehold of the Church began to loosen. Indeed, in some circles it even became rather trendy to deny the existence of God.

THE AGE OF REASON

The Age of Reason is the name given to the period, starting around 1650, that is marked by growing confidence in the power of human reason and in the possibilities offered by new scientific discoveries and ways of thinking. Also known as the (Age of) Enlightenment, it saw scepticism, science and intellectual rigour replace superstition, faith and a blind acceptance of classical authority. Thinkers considered instrumental in triggering the Age of Reason are Spinoza, Voltaire, Newton and Locke. It had its beginnings principally in France and England, and spread from there to other European centers and to America.

The Scottish philosopher David Hume (1711–76) was one of the first philosophers to deny the existence of God openly. Hume was an arch-sceptic and rejected anything that could not be gathered from personal sensory experience. That certainly meant throwing the baby Jesus out with the bathwater. The bathwater was a slop that included the existence of the self, logical necessity, causation and the validity of inductive knowledge itself. In Hume's *Dialogues Concerning Natural Religion* (1779) the sceptical character Philo puts forward objections to all the main arguments that are said to demonstrate the existence of God. Hume was slightly too early with his provocative stance, which is why the work was first published three years after his death.

By the time the German philosopher Friedrich Nietzsche (1844–1900) was writing, denial of God might have been

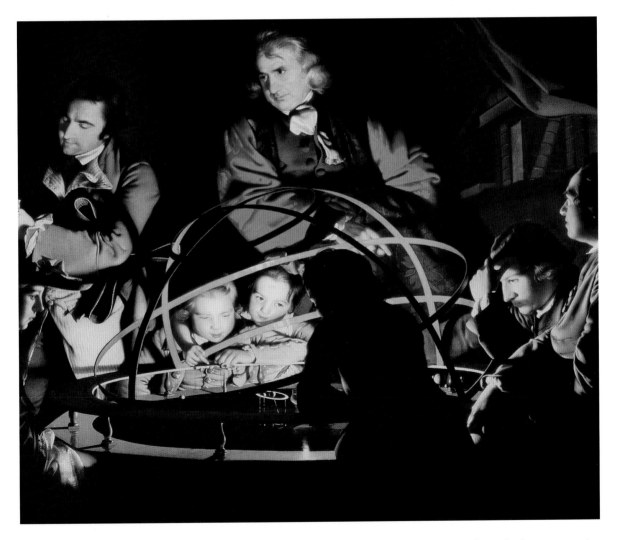

The Age of Reason saw a growing interest in science and the development of the scientific method.

> *"Religion is the sigh of the oppressed creature, the heart of a heartless world, and the soul of soulless conditions. It is the opium of the people."*
>
> Karl Marx, *German–French Annals,*
> written with Arnold Ruge (1844)

unpopular but was no longer as dangerous as it had been for Spinoza. Nietzsche's father, a Protestant minister, died when his son was just four, and the boy was brought up in austere Lutheran piety by his mother and sister. He became especially hostile towards Christianity, which he labelled a "slave morality". By this he meant that it had grown out of the bitterness and resentment of the oppressed and weak. Instead of tackling their low status in society or having the inner strength to master their resentment, they invented a scheme in which their oppressors would be punished in some imagined future life, providing the revenge that the weak were unable to take in the present life. In a slave morality, according to Nietzsche, the oppressed (slaves) denigrate the qualities or characteristics that give others power over them and elevate the opposite characteristics. So wealth and power are bad; poverty and humility are good. Those who demonstrate the bad attributes will be punished after death, and those who demonstrate the good attributes will be rewarded.

Nietzsche is not the only one to have seen religion as a distraction to keep the masses quiet. The German political philosopher Karl Marx's famous remark that religion is "the opium of the people" carries the same sentiment, except that instead of religion emerging from the oppressed consciousness he has it being force-fed to the proletariat by the establishment.

Marx followed the claim made by philosopher and anthropologist Ludwig Feuerbach (1804–72) that human beings had created God in their own image and that worshipping God diverted them from enjoying their own human powers. He criticized Feuerbach, though, for failing to understand why people are lured into following religions. According to Marx, it is a sense of alienation in material life that drives people to seek solace in spiritual life. He saw this alienation occurring in two ways: alienation of labor and social alienation. The second of these is the failure of contemporary society to acknowledge and exercise the innate communal nature of people. Human beings exist as a community, and life is only possible because we can rely on a vast network of social and economic relations. He sees the need for community "deviously acknowledged" by religion, which creates a false idea of a community in which we are all equal in the eyes of God.

The civic state offers another illusion of community in which we are all equal in the eyes of the law. When people are truly emancipated and can realize a true form of community, religion will naturally wither away. The Russian anarchist revolutionary Mikhail Bakunin (1814–76) was even more anti-God, seeing him as the (imaginary) incarnation of pretty much all the ills ever visited upon humankind.

> *"The idea of God implies the abdication of human reason and justice; it is the most decisive negation of human liberty, and necessarily ends in the enslavement of mankind, in theory and practice."*
>
> Mikhail Bakunin,
> *God and the State* (1882)

Because God didn't exist, we created him

The Austrian psychologist Sigmund Freud (1856–1939) also believed God to be an invention of the human mind, but arising through personal need rather than political manipulation. He described religion as a necessary illusion that helps to restrain our sexual and destructive tendencies. It derives, he argued, from our longing for a father figure to "exorcize the terrors of nature . . . reconcile men to the cruelty of Fate . . . and compensate them for the sufferings [of] civilized life."

Non-realist rather than non-real

Another option, proposed by the German philosopher Georg Hegel (1770–1831), is to redefine God. Called the non-realist view of God, this states that God is not something that exists independently but is a way of talking about a set of moral or spiritual ideas. This view has been criticized as disguised atheism, and certainly needs a major overhaul of our definition of God and what religion offers. If God doesn't exist in any kind of separate "out there" sense, then nor does heaven or hell, and the existence or otherwise of miracles has no connection with religion. It is a view that has found favour with a number of modern thinkers, even including some members of the clergy.

Pick a god, any god

If we accept any of the arguments for the existence of God, we have a starting point for religion. But none of the "proofs" offered by the philosophers proves the existence of the very precise God each of them would like to promote. If we accept that there must be a First Cause, or there must be a Grand Designer, or

Mikhail Bakunin was a Russian revolutionary philosopher, considered by many to be the originator of anarchist theory. Anarchism holds the state to be undesirable in all its forms.

"To speak of God is to speak about the moral and spiritual goals we ought to be aiming at, and about what we ought to become. . . . The true God is not God as picturesque supernatural fact, but God as our religious ideal."

Don Cupitt, *The Sea of Faith* (1988)

According to the Old Testament, God gave humankind specific laws by which to live, handily inscribed on stone tablets for Moses to show the (mostly illiterate) Israelites.

God must exist because we can think of him, that does not give us any proof that the god which exists is the God of the Bible or the Qu'ran, or of any other specific religious tradition. This is precisely the problem with Pascal's pragmatic wager.

For an adherent of one of the standard main European religions – Christianity, Judaism and Islam – there is no argument to be had about belief in God, or particularly, about his nature. For other philosophers, though, this has been an issue.

What is God like?

Thales of Miletus sought a naturalistic explanation of the observable world. However, he still believed that God is the mind of the world, and infuses all things. Xenophanes (*c.*570–*c.*475 BCE) believed that there was a single deity that was "in no way like men in shape or in thought" but "caused all things by the thought of his mind."

These are clearly not the same as the Homeric gods – a bunch of anthropomorphized and often churlish or vindictive deities who meddled in human affairs (and had sex with humans) at every opportunity. The Ancient Greek philosopher Epicurus (341–270 BCE) also rejected the idea of interventionist gods. He left the first discussion of "the problem of evil", asking: "Is God willing to prevent evil, but not able? Then he is not omnipotent. Is he able, but not willing? Then he is malevolent. Is he both able and willing? Then how can there be evil?" Epicurus concluded that the gods had no interest in human affairs.

Around five hundred years later, the Egyptian-born philosopher Plotinus (*c.*CE 204–270) reinterpreted Plato's writings in a way that put a tripartite divinity at the center. This made him – and through him, Plato – immediately accessible to Christian tradition and made tenable Plato's position as an acceptable pagan in Christian theology. Plotinus is considered the father of neoplatonism. For centuries, Plato was known principally through Plotinus.

The first trinity

Plotinus" trinity comprised the One, the Intellect and the Soul. Unlike the Christian trinity, these are not of equal standing but are successive "stages" of contemplative being. The One, sometimes called "the Good" is beyond description and is the mystical, ineffable source of reality. Everything emanates from the One. Plotinus believed we could achieve union with the One or ultimate Being by means of contemplation. The Intellect is the "Nous", which corresponds to the

---

ARGUMENTS FOR RELIGIOUS TOLERANCE

The English philosopher and physician John Locke (1632–1704), writing in *Letters Concerning Toleration* (1689–92), gave three reasons for religious tolerance. First, mortal humans can't dependably evaluate the claims of different religions. Secondly, even if we could be sure of a true religion, belief cannot be compelled – the best that regulation could do is produce token compliance with a heavy burden of resentment. Thirdly, coercion would lead to more discord and violence than tolerance.

James Gillray's 1790 cartoon depicts the "Atheistical-Revolutionist" Richard Price. He was deemed "atheistical" because he was a Unitarian (he denied the tripartite nature of God) and a "revolutionist" because he supported American independence.

divine mind or reason, and is the first thing to emanate from the One. From this comes the World Soul, and from that individual souls and then matter. Everything, then, is in a hierarchical chain of creation extending downwards from the One, but everything at the same time is part of the One, having come from it.

The spread of Christianity and then Islam rather put an end to questions about the nature of God for more than a thousand years. When, in the Age of Reason, thinkers such as Spinoza and Voltaire challenged the prevailing dogma, the nature of God was again up for debate. The question

raised by Pascal's wager – which God to bet on – opened out from a matter of choosing between different flavours of Judeo-Christian religion or Islam into also offering the pantheistic, Geist-style God described by Spinoza. This God was not tied to any existing doctrine, and didn't have any interest in human affairs. In a way, it's a philosopher's God rather than a believer's God. There is no point in praying to or worshipping a god who is not interventionist or even interested. Such a deity doesn't answer Kierkegaard's need for an "idea for which I can live and die", and doesn't provide the foundation of a moral code or social structure. But such a deity is exempt from the one really crucial question that challenges philosophers who defend the existence of a supposedly benign, interventionist God: the existence of evil.

God and evil

The problem of evil – how evil can exist in a world created and overseen by an infinitely powerful and benign deity – was first raised by Epicurus writing 2,300 years ago. The problem of suffering is similar, but simpler in philosophical terms. Suffering can be explained as part of a bigger plan that we can't understand, or as a precursor to greater rewards after death. But evil is tricky. Why would an infinitely good God allow the existence of evil – or even create evil? Here are some of the answers philosophers have suggested:

Irenaeus (*c.*CE125–202) said that without evil in the world, it would not be possible for us to achieve moral good and love for God; the existence of evil is necessary for building our souls.

St Augustine argued that the occurrence of evil is a result of the Fall, but that evil does not exist *per se* – it is a deviance from

According to St Augustine, the evil that started with the Fall of Adam and Eve is the absence of good rather than the presence of its opposite.

or absence of good, just as blindness is not "something" but is rather a lack of sight. Adam and Eve chose to defy God and so chose not to be good. Others can make the same choice.

St Thomas Aquinas largely followed Augustine, adding that evil does not exist as an objective fact but as a subjective judgement. Things are only evil when judged in relation to other events, things or people. All things are innately good but may incidentally produce evil results, so the cause of all things – even evil – is good: "This is part of the infinite goodness of God, that He should allow evil to exist, and out of it produce good."

The religious reformers Martin Luther (1483–1546) and John Calvin (1509–64) both explained evil as the result of the Fall of Man. Both also believed in predestination, though, so the Fall was an inevitable part of God's plan (as were all subsequent evils). God's plan is not understandable by humankind.

Gottfried Leibniz (1646–1716), best known now as a mathematician, argued that God has created the best possible world and so any flaws are inevitable in all possible worlds. He claimed that moral and physical evil (sin and suffering respectively) are the consequence of imperfect humans operating with incomplete understanding and exercising their free will in a sub-optimal manner. Some evil is necessary to make the "best possible" world, as virtues such as courage and morality cannot have meaning or even exist if there is no danger or evil as their counterpoint. God has to do a tricky trade-off between good and evil to get the "best possible" solution.

The British cleric Thomas Malthus (1766–1834) argued that evil exists to spur humankind to hard work and virtuous behaviour as a way of escaping hunger and poverty: "Evil exists in the world not to create despair, but activity."

Debate about the problem of evil continues. People of faith are often satisfied with the "it's a mystery" line, but for philosophy that's not really good enough. The best solutions seem to be either that there is no God or that the definition of God is wrong – he is not both infinitely good and infinitely powerful. But then that means "God" as we have defined him doesn't exist and either something else does or nothing does.

THE BEST OF ALL POSSIBLE WORLDS

Leibniz's theory of the best of all possible worlds was the butt of Voltaire's satirical novel *Candide* (1759). In it, the naïve youth Candide meets a devastating string of catastrophes with blithe stoicism, putting his trust in the lesson of his tutor Panglos that he is living in the best of all possible worlds. But the degree of suffering to which Candide and his companions are subjected is too extreme for him to hold fast to this belief. Eventually he is disillusioned and resigned to spending his last days growing vegetables.

Martin Luther, shown here with a cardinal, sparked the Reformation and the emergence of Protestantism.

CHAPTER 3

What is it to be
HUMAN?

*"What a piece of work is a man, How noble
in Reason, how infinite in faculties, in form and
moving how express and admirable,
In action how like an Angel! In apprehension
how like a god, the beauty of the world, the
paragon of animals. And yet to me, what is
this quintessence of dust?"*

William Shakespeare, *Hamlet,*
(1599–1602)

*"Thou art the thing itself: unaccommodated
man is no more but such a poor bare,
forked animal as thou art."*

William Shakespeare, *King Lear,*
(1603–06)

What are you? A mind? A body? A mind and a body? A mind in a body? Do you exist at all? Why do you exist?

Do I/you exist?

It might seem pedantic to feel a need to prove you exist, but existence is a pre-condition of "being like" – there's no point trying to work out what it is to be human unless we are secure in our existence.

Many philosophers have rooted existence in consciousness. To be conscious of our existence is then deemed to be sufficient proof of it, as we have to exist in some form in order to be thinking about whether we exist. Aristotle wrote that "to be conscious that we are perceiving or thinking is to be conscious that we exist". St Augustine pointed out that we can't argue that we don't exist, because just having the argument proves us wrong – what is not there can't argue.

The Muslim philosopher Avicenna, or Ibn Sīnā, born in what is now Uzbekistan, devised a thought experiment while in prison. Known as the "floating man", it proposed that if a man came into being, suddenly, suspended in air with no sensory input from anything, including his own body, he would still be aware and could think. Avicenna's conclusion was that the very act of thinking and being self-conscious would prove to that man that he existed. In addition, the thought experiment shows that the mind or soul is separate from the body as it can act without any inter-relationship with the body. The first awareness that the floating man/mind would have would be of its own existence, or its essence. This self clearly doesn't depend on any physical body, so the mind and body are separate and the mind is immaterial.

The most famous statement of the proof of existence is René Descartes" *cogito ergo sum*: "I think, therefore I am" (and also "I doubt, therefore I think, therefore I am"). It is pretty much the same as Aristotle's and Augustine's position, but the short version is snappier as a sound bite. Kant's version of the same argument was more long-winded, but says the same.

Even with all these authoritative philosophers and common sense on the side of our existence, there have been those who have doubted the proof of it. Some critics point out that thinking only proves that the "I" thinks, not that the "I" exists. As the Finnish philosopher Jaakko Hintikka (born 1929) has pointed out, if the statement were wrong, we would be left with an impossibility: "I don't exist, but I'm still wrong" – you can't be wrong if you don't exist. The French philosopher Pierre Gassendi (1592–1655) pointed out that the thinking only demonstrates the existence of the thinking itself – that thinking is happening. Friedrich Nietzsche, Søren Kierkegaard and David Hume all made the same point. It is too big a leap to assume the existence of the "I" that Descartes

> "The reality of external objects does not admit of strict proof. On the contrary, however, the reality of the object of our internal sense (of myself and state) is clear immediately through consciousness."
>
> Immanuel Kant, *The Critique of Pure Reason* (1781)

What part of us is it that makes us want to create art, and able to appreciate and be moved by art?

is laying claim to. Recognizing the existence of thoughts is no evidence that one is any particular thinker – the thinker of "I think, therefore I am" could as easily be a tadpole as Descartes, and he might be wholly deluded in his sense of personal identity.

But Kierkegaard's argument was not that Descartes didn't exist, simply that the logic was a bit circular. We have to presuppose a thinker exists to do any thinking, so taking the thinking as evidence of existence is not acceptable. The question comes back to what the "I" is. What or who are you?

21 GRAMS

An American physician, Dr Duncan McDougall (1866–1920), attempted to find the weight of the human soul. He weighed six elderly patients who were dying of tuberculosis and recorded an average weight loss at death of 21 grams. After conducting the same experiment with sheep, he claimed to see a slight increase in weight, and then a decrease – a result he explained by suggesting that a soul-portal arrived just before the departure of the soul and this briefly added to the mass of the body. The same experiment with dogs produced no variation in mass. He concluded from this that the human soul weighs around 21 grams and that dogs have no souls (although presumably sheep do).

His findings are not considered reliable.

Body and spirit

It must have occurred to people very early on that there is a distinct difference between dead people and living people. In dead people, something has gone. They are no longer animated (from *anima*, meaning spirit). They are lacking a soul, or whatever it is that we decide makes a person a living, thinking being. For thousands of years, people have made up stories or used religion to explain where the "being" part of dead people had gone. Perhaps it re-joined some universal One. Perhaps it hung around somehow, as a useful ancestor-spirit that might be able to intervene on behalf of the living. Perhaps it retained its personal integrity and moved on to another realm. Perhaps it was recycled, appearing in some new body, whether human or another creature. Or perhaps, most dismally, it just disappeared into nothingness. The dualism of mind and body, in various forms, emerged in cultures around the world and has been a persistent feature of religion and philosophy.

Religion thrives on the separation of the body and some kind of insubstantial soul or mind – the spirit being variously in control of the shell it inhabits or forced into sinful behavior by the body's depraved cravings. For philosophy, it raises various points of debate including where we should locate

This Dazu wheel of reincarnation (China, 1177–1249) depicts the Buddhist belief that the soul is reincarnated in a series of human and non-human bodies.

> *"What is it that, when present in a body, makes it living? — A soul."*
>
> Plato, *Phaedo*

what we call "I", and whether knowledge is more reliably arrived at through the physical senses or non-physical reason.

The mind/body problem

The mind/body problem is essentially this: what is the relationship between the mind and the body (or between physical and mental phenomena)? It is clear that there seem to be two sorts of state: physical and mental. Physical states and things are public – we can all see if someone is fat or thin, tall or short, for instance. Mental states are private: we can't tell what someone else is thinking or feeling (though we might gather clues from physical signs). Other questions spring from the over-arching mind/body question: what are physical and mental states? How can the mind affect the body or vice versa? What am "I" or where is "I", the person I think of as myself – mind or body? What is consciousness and how is it related to mind and body?

There are broadly three types of approach. The physicalist or materialist view is that everything is a physical state, even the mind. Idealists say all things are mental (for example, we construct the reality we experience). Dualists say that both physical and mental are real.

One, two or three parts?

In *Phaedo*, Plato considered humans to comprise three components: a soul, a mind

and a body. The soul is part of the Universal Being and is immortal. While we are alive, it is trapped in the body, along with the mind. The mind strives towards knowledge of the ideal Forms but the body is drawn to mundane sensual pleasures. It is the soul's job to try to guide body and mind to get them to work together, like a charioteer trying to steer a chariot by commanding the horse. It's a challenging task and rarely successful, so most people live lives that are dominated by their physical needs and desires.

A belief in ghosts presupposes a dualist model of human existence. After the death of the body, some kind of spirit or consciousness continues to exist.

For Plato, the soul is not material, and is not destroyed by death. Instead, it returns to the Universal Being and is later reincarnated in another being. It seems that this was not standard thinking before Plato; the audience to Socrates" pronouncements on the soul in *Phaedo* were surprised that he said the soul did not dissipate at the death of the body, like breath or smoke.

Nested souls of different ratings

For Plato's pupil Aristotle, the soul was the part of a being that was causally responsible for its animate activities. He saw a hierarchy of three types of soul, with the higher levels encompassing the lower levels. The most basic provides only the capabilities for nutrition and reproduction, the next level also provides for locomotion and perception, and the highest-ranking soul also has the capacity for thought. A bargain-basement soul could animate a plant; a medium-grade soul could animate an animal; but a human being needs a high-grade soul.

Aristotle saw the soul as inseparably linked with the body. It is what gives the body capacity to do things. The

Fictions such as Dr Jekyll and Mr Hyde, *and any number of werewolf stories, have their roots in the sense we have of conflicting urges – one towards the fulfilment of physical desires and the other towards a higher spiritual or rational mode of being.*

In Byzantine iconography, the soul is depicted as a bird trapped in a cage. The free bird has been released by death.

soul could not, in his view, survive the body's death, nor is it individuated in any interesting way. We each have separate souls as we are separate people, but all our souls are pretty much the same, just as each person's bones are pretty much the same. So although the soul is a different kind of material from the body, it was not an ethereal thing that could continue in independent existence, be recycled, or be held responsible for the virtuousness or otherwise of the ensouled individual.

For Aristotle, matter did not have properties of its own that were separate from the soul. How matter behaves depends on the Form it is in, and the Form is given by the soul. So one hunk of meat might be a human, and another hunk of meat might be an antelope – the material constituents are the same, but the soul (Form) is different.

Only slightly soulish

Epicurus took an even more physicalist view. He followed Democritus (*c.*460–370BCE) in believing that all matter consists of very tiny particles or atoms. The atoms of the soul, he said, were more agile than those of the body, but they were just as much physical entities. He made one important modification to Democritus" theory, though. According to Epicurus, atoms originally moved in parallel lines in the void but some, by an act of free will, swerved and bumped into others. These collisions gave rise to the different types of matter in the universe. (With the exception of the parallel lines, this is essentially the same position as modern physics – hydrogen atoms colliding produce first helium and then, in further combinations, other elements.) Extending his model to humans, Epicurus saw the soul as nothing more than the movement of atoms in the material body, but with the soul atoms freely swerving around. This unexplained property of atomic free will led to the free will humans enjoy.

With these three classical philosophers there is already a spectrum of theories about souls that ranges from an immortal soul distinct from the body, to something that is entirely physical and with only slight differences in form from the body. Although we no longer share Epicurus" view of the way matter works, his theory finds its modern counterpart in the belief that all thought, intentionality and personality come about only through the physical and chemical processes of neurology. Or, as French philosopher Maurice Merleau-Ponty put it in the 20th century, "I am my body."

The School of Athens by Raphael, painted 1509–11, shows Plato (center left) talking to Aristotle (center right).

The neoplatonic soul

The beliefs of the Ancients in this matter, as in so many others, filtered through to medieval and then Renaissance Europe in the writings of Plotinus and the early translators. Plotinus, as usual, adapted a Platonic view. He, too, took a tripartite approach, with the One at the top, the Intellect, coming next and the Soul placed below it. The Soul has two aspects: one that looks upwards or inwards towards the divine by means of the Intellect, and the other, outward-looking aspect that is Nature. Nature is responsible for the material world. The Soul corresponds to rational thought. The Intellect is the source of the archetypes or Platonic "Forms", and in its realm there is no distinction between thought and object, between perceiver and perceived. Plotinus describes the Intellect as being like the light of the sun: it illuminates the One, and is the means by which the One contemplates itself.

Both levels of Soul are present in humans, and it is up to us whether we

> "But what then am I? A thing that thinks. What is that? A thing that doubts, understands, affirms, denies, wills, refuses, and which also imagines and senses."
>
> René Descartes, *Meditations* (1641)

are preoccupied with the lower, bodily concerns of Nature or whether we devote our attention to the higher-level realities of the Intellect.

These three levels of reality, the One, the Intellect and the Soul, are levels of contemplation of a singular, eternal reality, not a progression through time. Nature creates time as a kind of fudge because it can't contemplate the divine. According to Plotinus, time comes about only in the lower order of existence because the Soul can't contemplate the ideal Forms directly, but only fragmented in objects perceived in a sequence of moments.

God kidnaps body and soul

With the emergence and growth of Christianity in Europe, the body and soul took on slightly different and more fixed forms. Thomas Aquinas, mediating as usual between Aristotle and Christian doctrine, took the Aristotelian model of the body consisting of both matter and Form with the soul providing the Form. But in keeping with Christian thought, he rejected Aristotle's idea that the body and soul were equally corruptible and dissipated on death. The Church taught that the soul survives death and is immortal.

Aquinas did not, though, think that

William Blake's depiction of the soul leaving the body shows them as two distinct entities (1808).

THE ARGUMENT FROM INDUBITALITY – A NIFTY TRICK

Descartes had a way of testing his ideas by thinking about which things he could doubt and about which things he felt secure. He decided that he could not doubt the existence of his mind, but he could doubt the existence of his body (he might just imagine it). As those things he doubted must be different from those things he did not doubt, it followed that mind and body must be different things.

---

the soul was pretty much the same as the person but without the body. On the death of the body, the personality and memories of that human being are lost. He followed contemporary Christian teaching in considering that on the Day of Judgement the body and soul would be reunited to form a whole person.

The "ghost in the machine"

Perhaps the most famous account of the split between the body and soul is so-called Cartesian dualism. René Descartes (1596–1650) believed that there are only two sorts of substance: mind and matter. (God was not considered to be any kind of substance.) These two substances have their own distinguishing characteristics. For matter, it is its physical extension in space – "thereness", we could say. For mind, it is the activity of thinking.

Further, Descartes argued that while the body is divisible, the mind is not. We can lose a leg, and our body still survives and exists, but we cannot have half a mind, or half a thought. John Locke tried to counter this by saying that we can be unconscious or asleep, and so then the mind is discontinuous. This

is not much of an argument, though, as he is citing discontinuity through time, whereas Descartes was talking about spatial divisibility.

Matter follows deterministic rules – it can't act at random. That physical laws govern the material universe was one of the defining discoveries of Descartes" age, and his own work on mathematics was part of it. The physical body, then, must work according to rules. Descartes came to see the body as a machine, controlled by the mind. But how would the mind, which has no substance, interact with the body – pulling the levers, as it were, to make it do things? Descartes decided there must be an organ that enabled this interaction and he chose the pineal gland – a small structure buried deep in the brain.

God gets in on the act

Even locating the mind (or soul) in an organ does not deal with the mechanism

---

"I am present to my body not merely in the way a seaman is present to his ship, but . . . I am tightly joined and, so to speak, mingled together with it, so much so that I make up one single thing with it."

René Descartes, *Meditations* (1641)

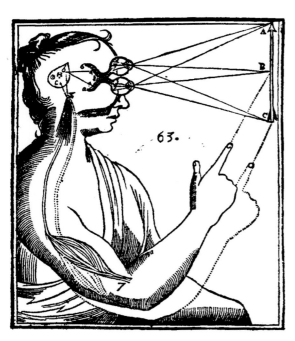

Descartes" model of how the mind and body interact. Light from an object travels to the eyes, where information is conveyed to the pineal gland, the part of the body that he believed was responsible for mediating between mind and matter. An instruction to move the hand can be initiated by the pineal gland.

of interaction. If the mind and body are different, with the mind utterly distinct from corporeal things, how, then, can one have any causal effect on the other? Clearly, our minds and bodies interact in some way: trapping a finger in a door makes us feel pain; when we choose to carry out a physical action, our bodies respond.

To solve the dilemma, the French philosopher Nicolas Malebranche (1638–1715) brought God in on the act (literally). God, Malebranche claimed, is the only causal power. The individual mind is a limitation of the one universal mind that is God. Our minds have no power to cause anything in the physical world. Nor do physical objects have the power to affect other physical objects, since in order to cause something to happen it's necessary to know how to cause it. In every case, God acts as an intermediary, causing a willed action to happen. It demands quite a lot of God, as he has to pay attention to everyone at all times, raising their arm or leg, closing their eyes, lifting a cup, whenever they require it. The mind and body are like two clocks, wound up by God and kept in time with each other by divine acts. This is the doctrine of *occasionalism*.

Although occasionalism seems to solve the problem of mind–body interaction, it has its own problems – not the least of which is the existence of God. Hume – who didn't believe in God anyway – mocked it as ridiculous, saying that if we can't even say how the human mind works, who are we to guess at how God's mind works?

Denying dualism

A thoroughly materialist view, in which the mind is seen purely as a product or aspect of the physical brain, solves the dualist problem by denying dualism. Spinoza's view was that mind and body are simply different ways of looking at parts of a single all-encompassing and homogenous whole. This gets rid of the problem by denying the separate existence of mind and body. The German philosopher Friedrich Schelling (1775–1854) came to a similar conclusion by a roundabout and confusing method that even Hegel had difficulty understanding, denouncing it as "All . . . a tangled mass of abstractions."

Hume took issue with Descartes" claim of indivisibility, saying that there is no reason

Conventional Christian thinking has the soul yearning towards God and the body often tramelling it with demands for physical gratification.

to suppose we have a unity of thought or perception rather than a diversity. We have lots of thoughts, dreams and perceptions, so under what pretext can we lump them all together and say the mind is indivisible? Rather than the self being a thinking thing, it is no more than a bundle of perceptions.

Indeed, even the term "bundle" implies a grouping together into some sort of unity.

Immanuel Kant replied to this argument by saying that it is necessary to presuppose an ego (a self) to do the perceiving, as otherwise the collection of "sense-data" that we interpret as seeing a tree or hearing the wind would just remain uninterpreted data – they would have no meaning. He pointed out that the mind could deteriorate, and there was no reason to suppose it could not or did not die with the body.

Gilbert Ryle (1900–76), who coined the term "the ghost in the machine" for Descartes" model of the mind piloting the body, dismissed dualism as a "category mistake", saying that mind and body were the same thing and that there is in fact no gap between mental acts and behaviors. Feelings are manifest in behavior, and the apparent separateness of feelings is only a construct of language. It comes about purely because of the way we use language to describe what is happening. He noted, too, that in dualist discourse the mind is always described in negative terms: non-physical, non-spatial, non-temporal, non-observable. If the body is clockwork, the mind is "not bits of clockwork . . . just bits of nonclockwork". He also observed that when we talk about mental or emotional states, what we are actually describing is a tendency to behave in a certain way. If we say someone is angry or sad, we expect or anticipate certain behaviors of them that demonstrate those emotions – we don't directly comprehend any inner state.

Are you now who you were before?

Wherever we think our identity is located, whether in a separate mind or in "bundles of perceptions", we all feel we are someone. Defining that someone and pinning it down can be difficult. The self is a slippery thing, prone to changing through time and with experience. In what ways do we stay the same person?

In *An Essay Concerning Human Understanding* (1689), John Locke proposed that it is the continuity of consciousness that determines identity. He did not root identity or continuity in the body, or even the soul: he said someone could be the reincarnation of Plato but would not *be* Plato, having no continuity of consciousness with Plato. It is on the basis of continuing consciousness, in the form of remembering what we have done and having enduring feelings and personality traits, that we can be said to remain the same person and can therefore be held accountable for acts we have committed in the past.

Hume, with his "bundle of perceptions" theory, had no place to locate the self. He believed the parts of the soul or consciousness are a commonwealth, or loose collection, of perceptions, thoughts, memories and opinions. Indeed, Hume even

---

PHILOSOPHERSPEAK: CATEGORY ERROR

Category errors can occur whenever a concept is misunderstood or misappropriated. An example would be to say there are three things in a field: two cows, and a pair of cows. Another would be to show someone around all the buildings that make up a university – the libraries, sports facilities, student housing – and then have them ask where the university itself is, as they have misunderstood the concept of "university".

John Locke (1632–1704) set out to investigate the mechanisms of human thought and understanding.

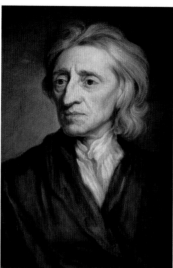

said that personal identity is a fiction. He also noted in the appendix to his *Treatise on Human Nature* (1739–40) that he was dissatisfied with his account of the self – but he never returned to it.

The Scottish philosopher Thomas Reid (1710–96) challenged Locke's account of personal identity being rooted in continuity through time with his "Brave Officer" argument:

'suppose a brave officer to have been flogged when a boy at school for robbing an orchard, to have taken a standard from the enemy in his first campaign, and to have been made a general in advanced life; suppose, also, which must be admitted to be possible, that, when he took the standard, he was conscious of his having been flogged at school, and that, when made a general, he was conscious of his taking the standard, but had absolutely lost the consciousness of his flogging."

According to Locke, the general must be the same person as the brave officer, and the brave officer must be the same person as the boy. But as there is no psychological connection between the general and the boy, they are not the same person. The strength of the argument lies in showing that Locke's position results in a contradiction, because the general both is and is not the same person as the boy who was flogged at school. The transitivity of identity is the principle that if A = B and B = C then A = C. But Locke's criterion of personal identity contradicts this rule; his criterion as either a necessary or sufficient condition of identity must be rejected.

The rise of the individual

Defining human identity in terms of either the mechanics of the body or its partaking of a great universal spirit does not accord with our personal experience of our identity. A revolt against these methods – both of which appear reductionist in different ways – began towards the end of the 18th century. The French-Swiss philosopher Jean-

---

THESEUS' SHIP

The Greek historian Plutarch described a paradox relating to a ship owned by Theseus. As parts of the ship wore out, they were replaced with new wood. Eventually, none of the original parts remained. Was it still the same ship?

Versions of the paradox referring to different objects have proliferated. The paradox can be applied to the human body: during the course of our lives, our cells are replaced over and over so that we are literally not the same person in terms of our physical being – yet we consider ourselves to be the same.

Jacques Rousseau (1712–78), and the German philosophers Arthur Schopenhauer (1788–1860) and Friedrich Nietzsche were among those who felt that human consciousness cannot

> "[The self is] that conscious thinking thing (whatever substance, made up of whether spiritual, or material, simple, or compounded, it matters not) which is sensible, or conscious of pleasure and pain, capable of happiness or misery, and so is concerned for itself, as far as that consciousness extends."
>
> John Locke, *An Essay Concerning Human Understanding* (1689)

be reduced either to parts of a body operating mechanically, or to a little parcel of an all-inclusive godhead or natural spirit.

What has become known as the Romantic movement tried to pull humankind out of the squalid, technology-oriented drudgery into which the Industrial Revolution had driven it and to reclaim the individual in philosophy. Nature and art were both considered the true home of the human spirit, the source of uplifting and liberating self-realization. The strong passions of the individual – the striving of the self, the passionate involvement with others, with nature and with God – were put at the center of the human experience.

The UK band the Sugababes formed in 1998. One by one, the original members left and were replaced so that by 2009 none of the original line-up remained. In 2011, the original trio formed a new band, but the Sugababes still existed.

The spirit of the Romantic movement is captured in this painting that shows the human, in contemplation of nature, as noble and triumphant.

Childhood: nurturing the new individual

Rousseau wrote some of the most important treatises on education and society of his time – perhaps of all time. He felt that the perfect condition of humans could be realized if allowed to flourish from childhood. His ideas on personal freedoms and social responsibilities lay at the heart of the French Revolution and the American Declaration of Independence.

It was Rousseau's belief that humankind was innately good and moral, but these qualities had been overlaid and corrupted by the nature of contemporary society. He advocated more natural (and universal)

education, with children taught morality initially and intellectual disciplines later on. In particular, education in religion should wait until the child was eighteen years old and so had developed critical faculties. Rousseau was not in favour of indoctrination or unexamined beliefs. Ironically, for all his fine intentions for everyone else, Rousseau sent four of his own children to an orphanage because he didn't want the bother or expense of raising them.

For Rousseau, contemporary society, industrialization, greed and science had all formed a crust of corruption over the natural nobility of humankind. A simpler life, closer to nature and focused on feeling and compassion, was the way for people to realize their potential and live the life they were born for. His two most important works, *The Social Contract* and *Émile*, were both published in 1762.

In *Émile*, he outlines a plan for the ideal education of a young person. He felt the process should be child-centered. The child should be brought up in the countryside, working under the guidance of a tutor who would allow the child to experiment but make sure the child is not harmed. Early education is concerned with emotions, with rational subjects not introduced until the age of 12. Rousseau argued that there was no virtue in the usual method of education, which required the child to use reason early on; if children could reason, they would not need to be educated. He also advocated that young adults learn a practical skill, such as carpentry, both for the benefits it offered and as a back-up in case of changed fortunes.

The German writer Johann Wolfgang

Perhaps following Rousseau's advice, Louis XVI was taught the skill of a locksmith. Sadly, his change of fortune was too extreme for a new life as a locksmith to be viable, and he was executed in the French Revolution.

von Goethe (1749–1832) is best known as a literary figure in the Romantic movement. But his work also had a significant effect on philosophy. A recurrent theme in his work was the tension between the passionate individual and the strictures of society. One of those he influenced was Schopenhauer, perhaps the most pessimistic philosopher of all time.

The will or won't

While Rousseau's view of human potential was highly optimistic, Schopenhauer saw the exact opposite. He regarded people as eternally hobbled by the driving force of the Will, a universal and perpetual striving that trapped and enslaved each individual.

Along with Kant, Schopenhauer considered the phenomenal (physical world) to be an illusion. He believed reality – the "thing-in-itself" – was actually the Will. This is manifested in all phenomena and beings as it has an insatiable urge to reveal itself in the world. We are all at the mercy of the Will, enslaved by its demands, and it is the cause of all our suffering. Schopenhauer believed the Will is revealed to the subjective self immediately and non-conceptually, though he never really explains what comprises this immediate awareness. It is hard to imagine just how gloomy the Schopenhauerian scenario is. He considered the world to be hell, with people playing the part both of damned souls and tormenting demons.

Schopenhauer felt that the way to escape from suffering was to conquer the Will and free ourselves from its rule. We can overcome it through contemplation of the arts (particularly music), through compassion and through religious contemplation and asceticism.

Art and music allow us to contemplate the universal Will separated from our own individual strivings, allowing a measure of objectivity. Compassionate engagement with another person leads us to recognize ourselves in them and them in us, and quietens the clamoring of the Will. The best source of peace, though, is religious fulfilment. A life of asceticism and meditation, denying the Will, leads to a blissful contemplation of nothingness. (Schopenhauer was the first Western philosopher to be heavily influenced by Eastern religions.)

Goethe's two-part poem Faust *addresses the issues of freedom and the individual's burning desire for knowledge and fulfilment. Faust makes a pact with the devil – his soul in return for knowledge. It took Goethe nearly 60 years to write (1773–1831).*

> *"To our amazement we suddenly exist, after having for countless millennia not existed; in a short while we will again not exist, also for countless millennia. That cannot be right, says the heart."*
>
> Arthur Schopenhauer,
> *The World as Will and Idea* (1819)

Schopenhauer maintained that recognizing our enslavement leads us to the realization that we should not fear death: it is the Will's desire to exist in the world of appearances that gives rise to our individual existence and, consequently, our suffering. As we are to resist the Will, Schopenhauer's argument seems to favour suicide in order to thwart the Will's evil plan. He tries to avoid this conclusion by claiming that as suicide is an act of Will it constitutes a surrender of the intellect: it is better to defeat the Will through contemplation.

SUPERMAN (WITHOUT TIGHTS)

Nietzsche was born near Leipzig, now in Germany, in 1844. His father, a Lutheran minister, died in 1849 and his baby brother the following year. Nietzsche, his mother and sister went to live with his father's parents. In 1864, while studying theology, Nietzsche lost his faith and turned instead to philology (the study of language). He then became interested in philosophy after reading the works of Schopenhauer in 1865 and consequently embarked on his own studies. After a brief spell in the army, Nietzsche was offered a professorship at the University of Basel when he was only twenty-four. He gave up his Prussian citizenship when he moved to Switzerland to take up his new post and remained stateless for the rest of his life.

In 1879, ill health forced Nietzsche to give up his academic post. He spent the next ten years as an independent author travelling around Europe. In 1889 he suffered a mental breakdown and remained severely mentally ill until his death in 1900.

Nietzsche became world-famous during the later years of his life, but his reputation was tarnished by the actions of his sister, who used his writings to further the Nazi cause. Elisabeth had split with her brother after marrying a man who held extreme anti-Semitic views. She moved with him to Paraguay to form Nueva Germania, intended as a model community built on the virtues of German culture and society. The colony was not a success.

Friedrich Nietzsche was one of the most profound and enigmatic philosophers in history. Unfortunately, he has also become one of the most controversial because of the way his ideas were used by the Nazis.

Her husband committed suicide and Elisabeth returned to Germany in 1893 where she slowly took control of her brother's literary legacy. Her corrupted version of Nietzsche's unfinished *The Will to Power* was later used, with Elisabeth's blessing, as evidence that Nietzsche sympathized with views later espoused by the Nazis. In fact he did not. Nietzsche was not a fan of anything German, and thought the term "German culture" was a contradiction in terms. When Elisabeth died in 1935, Hitler attended her funeral. Through her actions, Nietzsche's philosophy was brought into a state of disrepute from which it has still not fully recovered.

> *"O brave new world, That has such people in't."*
> *The Tempest,* William Shakespeare (1610–11)

Nietzsche was greatly influenced by Schopenhauer but did not share his extreme pessimism about humankind's destiny. He saw the Will not as a slave-master but as a strong force that could propel humans to greatness if allowed to achieve fulfilment. His concept of the *Übermensch* – "superman" or "beyond-man" – is similar to Aristotle's man of virtue. The *Übermensch* is the psychically strong human, not bowed down by the "moral slavery" of Christianity, who can forge new ideals and values by which modern (in the late 19th century) humankind could hope to step forward into a brave new world.

The *Übermensch* Nietzsche described in *Thus Spoke Zarathustra* (*Also Sprach Zarathustra*) (1883–85) is a goal humanity can set for itself, so that future generations will be superior. It's easy to see how this could be distorted by a regime that dreamed of a superior, elite master-race. The Nazis appropriated Nietzsche's term *Übermensch* and also introduced their own term, *Untermensch* (one never used by Nietzsche) for the underclass that could rightly (in their view) be enslaved or destroyed.

> *"[Nietzsche] had a more penetrating knowledge of himself than any other man who ever lived or was ever likely to live."*
> Sigmund Freud,
> founder of psychoanalysis

The personal person

Kierkegaard thought about the individual in a much more personal way. He rejected Descartes" dualism, and felt that arguing about whether reason or experience offered a better way of making sense of the world was to miss the point; neither takes account of the nature of a human being and the fundamental human condition. He was critical of Hegel and Goethe, and felt it was the task of philosophy to address how each person can live "as an individual". He saw humankind at each juncture as facing choices, having to make decisions, and lacking a way of making those choices. The quotation with which we started the book, as an explanation of the point of philosophy, was for Kierkegaard a statement of the dilemma of being human:

"What I really lack is to be clear in my mind what I am to do, not what I am to know . . . the thing is to find a truth which is true for me, to find the idea for which I can live and die."

This burden, which emerged again and again as a theme in Kierkegaard's writing, was also recognized by the existentialists. Indeed, Kierkegaard has sometimes been called the first existentialist. Certainly, in *The Concept of Anxiety* (1844) he dealt with the angst created by being aware that we have freedom to act, choices to make, but no guiding principle to help us choose. He developed a theory of three stages or competing life philosophies. The aesthetic is preoccupied with the here and now, with current pleasures and problems, and lacks commitment to anything greater. Despair follows when the aesthetic discovers the

Søren Kierkegaard grew up disillusioned and convinced bad things would happen to those around him. His mother and five of his six siblings died during his childhood.

reason, since if religious truths can be explained then there is no place for faith. For him, religion was an intensely personal thing, with God coming to each individual in an appropriate way.

Nietzsche is often considered the greatest of the Romantics, but as the 19th century gave way to the 20th it was not optimism that flourished as the legacy of the Romantic movement. The dour gloom of Schopenhauer and the confusion of Kierkegaard looking for a beacon in the confusion of angst laid a path towards existentialism – the movement that seized on the concept of humankind's essential solitude and hopeless search for meaning.

emptiness of such a life. The ethical person recognizes the importance of ideals, but is inevitably consumed with guilt when unable to live up to his or her own standards.

Kierkegaard had an answer, but one which the most ardent existentialists would reject: religion. His third stage, the religious, sees the individual wholly committed to transcendent ideals. He took religious belief to be an act not of reason but of faith. Indeed, he saw faith as the opposite of

> *"Each age has its characteristic depravity. Ours is perhaps not pleasure or indulgence or sensuality, but rather a dissolute pantheistic contempt for individual man."*
> Søren Kierkegaard

Edging towards existentialism

While Kierkegaard had prepared the ground for existentialism, it was Martin Heidegger (1889–1976) who planted the seed. In many ways, it was a natural follow-up to Romanticism, especially after Freud's insights into how the individual self is shaped by personal experiences, and the erosion of universal religious belief. Heidegger's insistence that we have to forge a life while facing our mortality marked a major turning point in 20th century philosophy. His *Being and Time*, published in 1927, had a huge impact on later thinkers in many spheres, most notably influencing the development of existentialism under Jean-Paul Sartre and deconstructionist criticism under the Algerian-French philosopher Jacques Derrida (1930–2004).

Existence before existentialism

The origins of existentialism lie in Heidegger's enquiries into *Dasein*, the "being that we ourselves are" or – literally translated – "being-there".

Vampires and other immortal beings would have a hard time in Heidegger's view. With life given meaning by its transience, the vampire could constantly put off until tomorrow what could be done today.

Heidegger saw *Dasein* as a self-conscious entity, aware of its own mutability: it knows that it is finite, mortal and will meet its inevitable fate. This awareness necessarily leads to angst or dread. But this is essential for life to have meaning. It is only if we are fully aware of our limited lives that we can live with authenticity and purpose. Self-awareness enables us to create a life from nothing, in the face of dread and death, referring only to purposes we have chosen for ourselves. (Heidegger's emphasis on choice is important.) It is an uncompromising and daunting view of life that has no room for a divinity offering purpose. Unlike earlier philosophers such as St Augustine and Kierkegaard, who

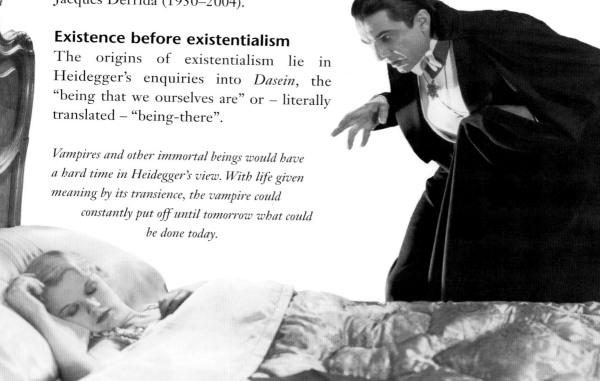

THE NAZI PHILOSOPHER: MARTIN HEIDEGGER (1889–1976)

Martin Heidegger was perhaps the most influential philosopher of the 20th century. But he was also – at least for a time – a Nazi, a fact that has complicated the way his ideas have been received.

As a philosophy student at the University of Marburg, Heidegger was influenced by and later employed by the philosopher and mathematician Edmund Husserl (1859–1938). On Husserl's retirement, Heidegger succeeded him as professor of philosophy at the University of Freiburg in 1928. Five years later, Heidegger became rector of Freiburg and joined the National Socialist German Workers" Party, or "Nazi" Party,

speaking in support of Hitler. He resigned as rector the following year, and his relationship with Nazism became more distant, but he remained a member of the Nazi Party until it was disbanded in 1945. He was banned from teaching between 1945 and 1949 and never allowed to resume his original professorship on account of his Nazi sympathies. Heidegger did not publicly renounce or apologize for his Nazi views, though privately he referred to them as "the greatest stupidity of my life". It is possible that while he allowed the official implementation of Nazi reforms, he secretly resisted them at least partially – there is no clear evidence either way.

believed that as individuals we "find" ourselves through God, Heidegger thought God irrelevant in philosophical terms. It is only the certain knowledge that we will die that gives our lives direction.

Human existence is defined by time, as past experiences and future hopes dictate who we are and what we do in a way that does not affect inanimate objects – their type of existence is static.

Heidegger distinguishes between authentic and inauthentic ways of living. An authentic life is one of our own choosing, which we build for ourselves. But we are free to choose the inauthentic, and Heidegger tries to say this is not a lesser choice. Authenticity is acting in the world, being a part of it on our own terms, defining ourselves. It is difficult to achieve while the

Dasein is immersed in the world, though. Luckily, anxiety (angst) is there to act as midwife. When *Dasein* is beset by existential angst, when the world suddenly seems bereft of meaning and we stare into the face of our inevitable demise, the world recedes. Then it is possible to be free (from the world and others) and to become ourselves.

It may seem perverse that the certainty of death is what frees us to make our lives. But imagine that you found an elixir of life that made you immortal. All your current ambitions lose their urgency. You might like to learn Arabic or become a politician. There is plenty of time. Today you can surf the web and dig the garden. There is no limit to the tomorrows in which you can achieve your ambitions, and no limit to the ambitions you can achieve – nor is there any great rush to achieve them. There is no need to choose or to know which things are important to you. The time-limitedness of life is what gives it purpose; the freedom to choose is forced upon us by mortality.

Although Heidegger would later deny that he was an existentialist, the principal motifs of existentialism are all first introduced in *Being and Time*: the "being there" of existence (the importance of the self-located in the world); the importance of the individual, especially in relation to the "crowd"; a preoccupation with *angst* (anxiety), death, and nihilism; the assertion that science can't provide a framework for understanding what it is to be human; the locating of "authenticity" in life in self-realization through choice. Existentialism rejects previous systems for categorizing human existence and asserts the primacy of the individual in defining ourselves – existence is more important than essence.

That sounds more complex than it is. Our individual actions define who we are;

SUPPORTING SCIENCE:
SIGMUND FREUD (1856–1939)

Sigmund Schlomo Freud was an Austrian psychologist and the founder of "psychoanalysis". This is based on the belief that certain early childhood experiences are repressed by the conscious mind. Generally, these experiences are related to sexuality, but they can be any type of experience the child thinks other people would criticize. The repressed memories later cause physiological disruptions and mental illness. Treatment involves getting the patient to revive and discuss the memories. Freud's ideas had a massive impact on Western thought and philosophy.

Not one to miss an opportunity to blow his own trumpet, Freud suggested that his psychology represented a new "Copernican revolution", claiming to have proven that the conscious mind, or the self, is not "master of its own house", as all rationalist and Cartesian philosophies supposed.

Existential angst is not just a teenage indulgence – according to Heidegger, it is the mood that frees us to live "authentic" lives.

those actions are freely chosen. Our essence therefore comes from our existence (in actions) rather than being predetermined by others (in the form of labels assigned by society) or by genetics. Carrying out kind acts defines someone as a kind person. Acting cruelly defines someone as a cruel person.

Gauloises and coffee in Paris

Jean-Paul Sartre, the poster-boy for existentialism in post-war France, drew heavily on Heidegger and Keirkegaard, but went far beyond them. In *Being and Nothingness* (1943) he produced a powerful and clear exposition that captured the spirit of an age. Sartre aimed to show that a person first exists without purpose or definition, then finds himself or herself in the world

and, as a reaction to experience, defines the meaning of life. This is a personal endeavour – it is up to each of us to choose the life we feel is best. It is the polar opposite of Aristotle's view that man is created for a purpose and must strive to fulfil that purpose. For Sartre, a person is defined by their actions. Someone who acts like a coward *is* a coward. But there is no innate nature that compels someone to be a coward, and he or she can choose to act bravely on another occasion, so becoming brave.

For Sartre, everything is a choice, even whether or not to believe in God (though he was himself an atheist). In answer to those, like Blaise Pascal or St Augustine, who claimed to have experienced a divine revelation or miraculous visions, Sartre says that it is still up to the individual to decide whether to believe they are revelations from God or merely hallucinations. The decision is personally made, and cannot be laid at God's door. Sartre denies the existence of compulsion, leaving the individual responsible for every action. Sometimes an action is a response or reaction to extreme circumstances, but even a constrained choice remains a choice and an exercise of personal power. A man with a gun pointed at his head can choose whether to obey a command or be shot. The dire consequences of a choice do not deny the existence of the choice.

Of course, the flipside of freedom is responsibility. If everything is freely chosen, we are entirely responsible for our actions. There is no opportunity to make excuses, to blame someone else or to shift it all onto God. Shirking responsibility like this is an act of "bad faith" and is self-deception.

Jean-Paul Sartre (center) and Simone de Beauvoir were part of a group of philosophers, writers and other intellectuals who regularly met and worked in cafés in Paris.

It is not easy to be the Sartrean individual. We are each encumbered by three burdens: anguish, abandonment and despair. "Anguish" arises from awareness of our responsibility. Our choices and actions serve as examples for the rest of mankind: each choice issues a statement to the world that this is how we believe life should be led. "Abandonment" follows from the recognition that God does not exist and that we are without help or guidance in moral matters: we have to make it all up as we go along. "Despair" is the state of acting without hope. We can't trust that things will turn out for the best, or put our faith in providence (which doesn't exist). Instead we ourselves are all we can rely on, and must tailor our acts and choices to bring about the outcomes we desire.

All this means that we are "condemned to be free". It is a weighty burden, but need not inevitably lead to pessimism and despair. Sartre says that existentialism involves a "stern optimism" in its message that "the destiny of man is placed within himself." In modern psychobabble, it's "empowering".

Existing and existentialism in society

Taking up Sartre's conviction that as individuals we are self-determining, and can't lay the responsibility for what we are on anyone or anything else, the French philosopher Simone de Beauvoir (1908–86) explored the role that society and context must play in helping to define personhood. In *The Second Sex* (1949), de Beauvoir accepted that the individual is born free but pointed out that gender inevitably pushes women into particular moulds that vary between societies. Each woman "becomes" what the term "woman" means in her own social context, whether that is domestic goddess,

> *"One is not born, but rather becomes, a woman."*
> Simone de Beauvoir, *The Second Sex* (1949)

career woman, temptress, supermum or anything else. The female becomes a woman by accepting and living the role that society defines as appropriate for her.

Sartre would have said that acting in accordance with someone else's expectations and then blaming them for what we become is an act of "bad faith". But de Beauvoir insisted that "bad faith" presupposes an awareness of the possibility of choice and so for the potential for freedom. This is not always the case. Children cannot

act in bad faith because their actions are constrained by parents or guardians – they don't have the freedom to choose how to be. At adolescence they reach an "awakening" when existentialist angst takes hold. Women have, historically, been similarly constrained according to de Beauvoir: socio-economic circumstances have defined their existence and they have been unaware of the potential for freedom. Consequently, they are not acting in bad faith in becoming the women that society expects them to be.

The Physical Impossibility of Death in the Mind of Someone Living *by Damien Hirst: Heidegger maintained that only the certainty of death gives life any meaning – the "possibility of impossibility".*

Albert Camus was not only a philosopher, he was also a keen soccer player. He once said, "What I know most surely about morality and the duty of man I owe to sport."

Simone de Beauvoir has become something of a feminist icon. Many of the ideas she expressed in *The Second Sex* and *The Ethics of Ambiguity* (1947) have become central to the feminist movement: that women must recognize their own freedoms, define their own being, and free themselves from the "enslavement" of a society whose rules and values are defined by men.

How can we bear it?

The engodded – those who accept there is a god, whether or not they struggle with their faith – have little cause or excuse for existential angst. Either their purpose in living is clear, or it is a great mystery they may not enquire into. But for the unengodded, the question "Why am I here?" is one that can be too hard to face. At least, the answer – "no reason" – can be too hard to accept. The crisis of being, of knowing why we have being, is only really possible for those who don't believe in a god. Existential angst is a feature of the 20th century. But existentialism covers more than teenage agonizing about existence.

> *"There is only one truly serious philosophical problem, and that is suicide."*
> Albert Camus,
> *The Myth of Sisyphus* (1942)

The French-Algerian writer and philosopher Albert Camus (1913–60) was an existentialist and friend of Jean-Paul Sartre in Paris until the pair fell out in 1951 and never spoke again. His most important work of existentialist philosophy, *The Myth of Sisyphus* (1942), deals with the theme of "absurdity". Camus claims that human existence is absurd as we attempt to make sense of a senseless world. He used the Greek hero Sisyphus as an illustration of the futility and hopelessness of all human endeavour. Sisyphus is condemned by the gods to push a boulder up a hill for all eternity, only to have it roll back down as soon as he reaches the summit. Similarly, we all spend our lives achieving nothing.

The inevitable consequence of pondering the desolate pointlessness of existence is to ask "Why should I not commit suicide?" Camus considers that other writers and philosophers of an

> *"All the labour of the ages, all the devotion, all the inspiration, all the noonday brightness of human genius, are destined to extinction in the vast death of the solar system, and the whole temple of man's achievement must inevitably be buried beneath the debris of a universe in ruins."*
> Bertrand Russell

existentialist bent, including Husserl, Kierkegaard, Sartre and the German psychiatrist Karl Jaspers (1883– 1968), have all shied away from this conclusion. Instead of keeping faith, they have tried to resolve the conflict between the rational human being and the irrational world. But this conflict cannot be resolved, and suicide is just another attempt at resolution. We are all backed into a corner. If we accept the position of absurdity, we have to accept death. If we refuse it, we live teetering on the precipice, looking into the abyss: we exist in full knowledge of both our mortality and the futility of all we do in our lives. Camus advocates "revolt" – accepting awareness of the situation without being resigned. Suicide would be a defeat, a denial of the condition of our existence. According to Camus, "The struggle itself is enough to fill a man's heart. One must imagine Sisyphus happy."

Sisyphus was condemned forever to push a boulder uphill as a punishment for deceitfulness.

Back to the machine – but with no ghost

The removal of God or any kind of supernatural or ethereal spirit from the consideration of the human leads us back to a physicalist view – we have Descartes" machine of the body, but with no ghost to animate it. This is the position adopted by the American philosopher Daniel Dennett (born 1942). He rejects the idea that the mind is a separate, disembodied entity, arguing that all aspects of ourselves can be explained by looking at how the brain works. Personality, intellect, opinions, thoughts, dreams – everything is reducible to neurology. He describes the brain as a "semantic engine", a mechanism for extracting meaning from the world.

Denying that there is anything inherently special or mystical in consciousness, Dennett maintains that there is no quantifiable and real difference between something that

---

PHILOSOPHERSPEAK: THE ABSURD

Absurdism holds that there is no meaning in what happens in the world. It is the opposite of a belief in karma (that good things will happen to people who act well). The absurdist holds that the world itself is amoral: anything can happen to anyone, irrespective of their own moral standing or behaviors. Absurdism is not really compatible with Christian faith, as it allows of no overarching, invisible purpose or direction.

seems conscious and something that *actually is* conscious – so a computer can have consciousness. As computers become better able to do things we currently associate only with human intelligence – such as tell jokes or write poetry – the distinction between real and artificial intelligence, between genuine consciousness and mimicked consciousness, will become less and less meaningful until it has to be abandoned. Indeed, Dennett has said that even thermostats have "beliefs" about the world. A thermostat behaves on the basis of assumptions about the world that can't be distinguished from beliefs, in that they have the same effects as beliefs. Dennett sees the brain as nothing more than a very sophisticated computer, and the mind as the product of Darwinian evolution.

Dennett's view that the brain is very like a computer is refuted by another American philosopher, John Searle (born 1932), a pioneer in cognitive science. The view that computers can be conscious, which Searle terms "strong AI" (artificial intelligence), is challenged by a thought experiment he called "the Chinese Room" (*see panel opposite*).

Human minds are distinguished from computers, according to Searle, by intentionality. Computers are defined syntactically, in terms of formal symbol manipulation, and that, he argues, is insufficient to imply consciousness.

Consciousness emerging

So, if consciousness is not something that can be experienced by a computer, what is it exactly, and how does it emerge? In his theories about the mind and consciousness, Searle rejects Cartesian dualism – that the mind is something non-physical and separate from the body. He also rejects the reductionism of thinkers such as Dennett, who believe that consciousness can be reduced to a series of physical processes in the brain.

Instead, Searle takes a position that he calls biological naturalism. Consciousness is an emergent property of the brain. He uses the analogy of water to explain the idea. Wetness is an emergent property of water that is brought about by the behavior of water molecules *en masse*. No individual molecule is "wet"; the wetness is a feature of the whole system of molecules and the way they behave when water is in its liquid form. In the same way, one cannot point to a neuron and say "this one is conscious". Consciousness emerges as a result of the whole system. Events at the micro-level – perhaps at the level of individual neurons – cause a phenomenon that at the macro-level we call consciousness.

Some have seen biological naturalism as a form of dualism since micro-level properties can be objectively studied by, for example, a brain surgeon, but the brain surgeon cannot in the same way access macro-level properties such as pain, desire or joy. Searle rejects this suggestion. He stresses that consciousness is a type of physical property; it is not something separate like a kind of juice that is squirted out by the neurons. It is the state that the system is in – part of that system and inseparable from it. How it works – how micro-level behavior creates consciousness at the macro level – is a question for the neuroscientists. But as a problem for philosophy, Searle regards it as solved.

THE CHINESE ROOM ARGUMENT

Imagine you are in a room with an enormous rule-book, which allows you to look up Chinese sentences and tells you how to respond to them in Chinese. Through a hole in the wall, someone passes a piece of paper with a question written on it in Chinese. Using the rule-book, you look up the answer, write it down in Chinese, and pass it through another hole. To the people outside the room you seem to understand Chinese, whereas in fact you have no understanding of the language at all.

The Chinese Room is an analogy for artificial intelligence. The rule-book is the equivalent of a computer program, which manipulates data according to a set of rules, and produces answers. It can give the appearance of being intelligent, but is not. A computer model of the mind is not actually conscious, argues Searle, just as a computer model of the digestive system cannot actually eat pizza. A computer that can model falling in love or reading a novel or getting drunk does not actually experience these things, but produces a simulation of the processes involved.

If a robot can ever be said to develop consciousness, will that mean that we have moral responsibilities towards it and must treat it ethically? If a robot can feel pain or sorrow, are we allowed to treat it as a slave?

CHAPTER 4

What can we **KNOW?**

> "[The soul is] a veritable prisoner fast bound within his body . . . and that instead of investigating reality by itself and in itself it is compelled to peer through the bars of its prison."

Plato,
Phaedo

> "To say something is meaningful is to say that that is how we arrange it so; how we comprehend it to be, and what is comprehended by you or I may not be by a cat, for example. If a tree falls in a park and there is no-one to hand, it is silent and invisible and nameless. And if we were to vanish, there would be no tree at all; any meaning would vanish along with us. Other than what the cats make of it all, of course."

William Fossett,
Natural States (1754)

We receive information about the world through our senses – but is it reliable?

Outside the existence of our own minds, what can we be sure of? Do you see blue in the same way that I do? Is the Sun really hot and round? Sometimes, things that look obvious are deceptive – the Sun and Moon look about the same size. But then methods of investigation other than the evidence of our own senses can reveal an error in our common-sense assumptions. The branch of philosophy that deals with knowledge is called epistemology.

> ### KNOWING THAT AND KNOWING HOW
>
> Philosophers distinguish between different types of knowledge.
>
> **Knowledge that** or propositional knowledge is of most concern to epistemology. It is concerned with – for instance – knowing that 10 x 10 = 100 or knowing the laws of physics.
>
> **Knowledge how** is concerned with acquired skills – such as knowing how to multiply numbers, or how to ride a bicycle.
>
> **Acquaintance knowledge** is concerned with knowing a person or a place.

What makes you think you know?

How can we know things? The quality of knowledge and how we can attain certainty has puzzled philosophers for 2,500 years. In brief, there are three possible ways of knowing things:

▶ The evidence of our senses – we know some things by experience, by the processing of sense-data such as what we see and hear. You might be certain your desk exists because you can see it and touch it.

▶ Reason – through reasoning, or a logical sequence of thoughts, you might be persuaded of the truth of a proposition such as "the area of a square increases by four if you double the length of the sides".

▶ Innate belief – you might believe that you have a soul or that God exists because you have a strongly held conviction that this is the case.

How far each of these methods can be trusted has long been debated.

Can we be sure?

The Greek philosopher Xenophanes was the first person known to have been cautious about claims of certainty. Anticipating Socrates, he said that even if we do discover the truth we have no way of ascertaining that what we have discovered is actually correct, and that things are as we think they are. Even so, philosophical inquiry is still useful. It can reveal errors and tell us what is not the case even if we can't be certain of what is the case.

Socrates, who was born in Athens in 470BC, around the time that Xenophanes died, often claimed that the only thing he could be certain of was his own ignorance. A good deal of his teaching consisted of asking his audience to give definitions of common concepts such as "beauty" or "piety", then showing by reasoned argument that whatever answer they gave fell down under scrutiny, turning out to be absurd or paradoxical. Through this, he intended to show how dangerous it is to accept established ideas uncritically. He frequently demolished in

SOCRATES (470–399BCE)

Socrates was an itinerant philosopher who wandered around his home city of Athens, teaching philosophy through discourse and oratory. He served as a soldier in the Peloponnesian War (431–404BCE), then became embroiled in the political turmoil that followed the war, before turning to stonemasonry work and raising a family. He inherited enough money from his father, a sculptor, to be sufficiently financially independent to pursue his interest in philosophy. Socrates later turned to investigating the development of moral character. He spent the latter years of his life debating with the aristocratic youths of Athens, often to the annoyance of their parents. He refused any payment for his teaching, and his young followers were often fiercely loyal to him.

He was something of a maverick, and soon antagonized all the citizens of Athens. He challenged their automatic belief in received ideas and wisdom, encouraging them to think critically. The citizens accused him of corrupting the minds of the young, and of not believing in the gods, and put Socrates on trial. His argumentative response to the accusations did not help his case, and when he was asked to suggest a suitable punishment for himself he recommended that he be allowed free meals in the public dining hall. This further angered the judiciary. He was offered a reprieve if he agreed to give up teaching philosophy, but he refused and was sentenced to death. He died in 399BCE by drinking hemlock, surrounded by his friends and followers.

Socrates taught through debate, and left no written works. What we know of his methods and ideas comes from the writings of his contemporaries and his pupil Plato. Socrates is considered the originator of Western philosophy, the first philosopher to pursue wholly philosophical and metaphysical enquiry.

Socrates refused exile and drank the hemlock-based poison provided for his execution. Plato reports in Crito *that one injustice (execution) does not excuse another (escape) – even when* Crito *says that Socrates has a moral duty to avoid orphaning his children.*

argument anyone who claimed to have certain knowledge of something. His method, known as "socratic dialogue" or "dialectic", lies behind the current practice in philosophy and other disciplines of continual critical reflection.

Two approaches to knowing

Just as Socrates was the teacher of Plato, so Plato was the teacher of Aristotle, placing three of the greatest thinkers in a direct line of intellectual descent. This wonderful accident of history determined the direction of Western thought for two millennia.

Putting trust in reason

Plato took up the issue of what we can know and how we discover it, and pursued it along the rationalist lines set out by Socrates. It follows from Plato's theory of Forms that if what we perceive as the real world is but a shadow of the perfection it mimics, we cannot attain true knowledge through our senses. If we can't trust our senses to reveal truth, what can we trust? The answer Plato gives is "reason".

In *Meno*, Plato presents a dialogue between Socrates and Meno, a wealthy young general who has just arrived in the city with a large retinue of slaves. Socrates

and Meno are debating what virtue is and whether it can be taught. The dialogue contains Meno's paradox. Meno, confused by what Socrates is saying, asks: "How can

---

HOW ARE WE TO KNOW PHILOSOPHY?

There are different ways of presenting philosophical ideas (or any ideas). Some of the important have been:

Socratic debate or Platonic dialogue: presenting two different points of view and exploring them through a dramatized dialogue or dialectic. The preferred point of view can be given the more persuasive arguments and defeat the opposing view or both can be given with equal conviction, leading the listener to consider and decide the merits of the case. As a method of teaching, the point is to develop the student's skill rather than to win him or her over to a particular point of view.

Logical syllogisms, as used by Aristotle: beginning from one statement, logic is used to demonstrate that other propositions necessarily follow from it.

Aphorisms, as presented by Marcus Aurelius in his *Meditations* (CE170–180): concise, memorable expressions of thought. No argument is presented; the aphorism stands or falls on its own perceived merits.

Thesis/antithesis, as presented by Thomas Aquinas: Aquinas presents his arguments in the *Summa Theologica* by first stating the question, then presenting the antithesis with its supporting arguments, followed by the thesis (preferred answer) with its supporting arguments and finally refuting the arguments in favour of the antithesis with strong counter-arguments. Hegel added "synthesis" as the new position that comes out of comparing a thesis and antithesis and moving on to new knowledge.

Propositions, as presented by Ludwig Wittgenstein (1889–1951): a series of statements presented in such a way that the logical progression from first to last forms a compelling argument.

Aspasia, the Athenian socialite and consort of Pericles, was renowned as a conversationalist; philosophers, including Socrates, attended what now are called salons at her home.

you look for something when you don't know what it is? Even if you find the thing, how will you know that what you have found is the thing you didn't know?"

Socrates restates this as: "[A] man cannot search either for what he knows or for what he does not know. He cannot search for what he knows – since he knows it, there is no need to search – nor for what he does not know, for he does not know what to look for."

He goes on to try to demonstrate to Meno that knowledge is *a priori* – pre-existing. The soul is immortal and has been exposed to knowledge before it inhabits the body that, with some prompting, it remembers during life. Socrates attempts to demonstrate this using one of Meno's slaves. The slave does not at first know a geometrical formula, but through questioning him, Socrates eventually gets the boy to state the formula. Socrates claims that as he has taught the boy nothing, this is proof that the boy is remembering *a priori* knowledge. (Of course, it is no such thing – the boy applies his reason to the problem and so solves it. He can do this when Socrates prods him

---

PHILOSOPHERSPEAK: RATIONALISM

Rationalists believe that knowledge can be discovered purely by the application of reason. Knowledge does not need to be – and cannot reliably be – grounded in our experience of the world around us.

---

in the right direction with his questions.) The final outcome of the dialogue is that knowledge is "justified true belief". This definition was widely accepted until 1963, when the American professor of philosophy Edmund Gettier (born 1927) pointed out that sometimes a justified true belief would not count as knowledge. This can happen when a person has a justified belief that happens to be true only by chance. For instance, a woman in love with a man with ginger hair believes she will marry him and so believes her future husband will have ginger hair. In fact, she splits up with this man and marries someone else who also,

by chance, has ginger hair. Her belief was justified, and turned out to be true, but was not knowledge.

Plato presented his philosophical ideas through a series of dialogues in which Socrates debates with others, so stepping through the arguments that lead to his conclusions.

Champion of the senses

The star pupil of Plato's Academy must have been Aristotle. He took issue with the theory of Forms and came out on the side of empirical evidence, championing what we can learn about the world through our senses. The basis of the scientific method is in Aristotelian *empiricism*: he taught that a thorough and methodical investigation of the world, including qualitative comparisons and assessments, can yield knowledge about phenomena. These phenomena, according to Aristotle, represent true reality, and not some shadowy, cheap version of a reality we can never truly apprehend.

Taking it all with a pinch of salt

The Greek philosopher Sextus Empiricus (*c.*CE160–210), left eleven volumes of philosophy in which he set out the doctrine of the Pyrrhonian Sceptics. These books are the only source on the Sceptics, and we know little of Empiricus himself. The Pyrrhonian Sceptics were a group founded around the 3rd century BCE by Pyrrho (360–270BCE), a philosopher who, like Socrates, wrote nothing himself. The central claim

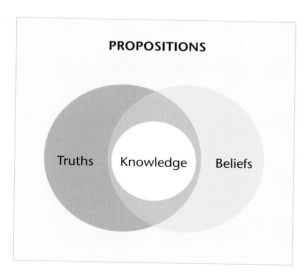

PROPOSITIONS

Truths — Knowledge — Beliefs

The area of overlap between the set of true things and the set of beliefs includes, but is not limited to, knowledge.

PLATO (c.427–347 BCE)

Plato was born into a noble family, probably in Athens. He had two brothers and a sister, but we know little else of his early life. He was a pupil of Socrates, and in his own writings he presented his philosophical ideas in the form of dialogues between Socrates and others. It's thought that Plato may have travelled in Italy, Sicily, Egypt and Cyrene (Libya), and returned to Athens at the age of 40. There he set up the first known organized school or college in the Western world, called the Academy. It continued as an educational establishment until it was destroyed in 84 BCE. One of Plato's pupils at the Academy was Aristotle.

Plato often said that his purest philosophy was never written down and he shared it only orally with close and trusted friends and colleagues. He said the written word was not an appropriate medium for important and difficult material as it could not be explained or defended in the author's absence.

Plato left important, influential writing about metaphysics (the nature of reality) and epistemology (what we can know of it), politics and ethics.

Plato (c.427–347 BCE), the pupil of Socrates and teacher of Aristotle, was one of the greatest philosophers who ever lived.

of the Sceptics is that we can't assert any proposition with more certainty or justification than we can assert its opposite. Pyrrho's philosophy is summed up in the saying "No more this than that". So we can be no more certain that, say, time runs relentlessly forward than that it does not.

How does this work? The same object can look very different from a distance and when viewed up close, but there is no good reason to suppose the closer view is more truthful than the distant view. A forest, for instance, can only be seen from a distance whereas, close to, we can't tell whether it is merely a stand of a few trees. The gap between reality and appearance cannot be closed, because what we "know" of reality we learn through our fallible bodily senses. It is not possible to say with certainty that one thing is more likely to be true than another.

> "The safest general characterization of the European philosophical tradition is that it consists of a series of footnotes to Plato."
>
> Alfred North Whitehead,
> *Process and Reality* (1929)

From this viewpoint it is not possible to tell whether you are looking at a few trees or a forest that extends for many miles.

The intention of scepticism is to bring a comforting and calming disengagement from frantic questioning. But it can as readily lead to anxiety or apathy as, if no knowledge is secure, what's the point of pursuing it? Empiricus, though, says that scepticism should lead to tranquillity and peace of mind, and these are the ultimate aims of sceptical philosophy.

Suppose we decide that some things are definitely good (say, health and a close family) and others are bad (say, poverty).

- ► We will be resentful if bad things come to us and good things do not. But if we benefit from the good things we will be anxious about losing them.
- ► The sceptic, on the other hand, does not make a judgement about what is good or bad, right or wrong, and so on. Instead, the sceptic does not hanker after or avoid anything with great passion, but remains indifferent to changing fortune, and so lives a tranquil life.

Of course, it is hard to live like this. Critics of scepticism point out that the claim is self-defeating. If we really can't assert one proposition over its opposite, the same is true of the sceptical claim itself – we can't say we should live

---

PHILOSOPHERSPEAK: EMPIRICISM

Empiricism is the belief that empirical reality is accessible to the physical senses and can be measured, observed and known through direct interaction with the world.

like this with any more certainty than we can say that we should not live like this.

Knowledge through faith

With the coming of Christianity, a new conduit for knowledge appeared in the form of an omniscient God. St Augustine saw both philosophy and religion as quests for truth, though with religion seeking a truth of a higher order. At the heart of his philosophy was the belief that wisdom can ultimately be attained only through faith. Although some truths could be reached through reason alone, he felt that faith was necessary for true understanding, and returned repeatedly to a text from the Bible: "unless thou believe thou shalt not understand" (Isaiah: 26:3). Augustine did not arrive at this conclusion lightly. As a young man, he renounced religion but, after converting in his early thirties, set about showing that reason could prove the tenets of faith.

The scientific revolution

Until the 16th century, the Western world lived in the shadow of the Classical period. Then at some time around 1550, during the Renaissance in art and the humanities, a clutch of scientific advances led to a reassessment of mankind's place in the universe. It is impossible to overstate the impact of this change. In place of superstition, reverence for the authority of the ancients and blind faith, a spirit of enquiry, investigation and challenge led people to pursue truth through scientific means. The scientific writings of Aristotle, as well as those

> *"How could the Earth hang suspended in the air were it not upheld by God's hand? By what means could it maintain itself unmoved, while the heavens above are in constant rapid motion, did not its Divine Maker fix and establish it?"*
>
> John Calvin,
> *Commentary on Psalms* (1557)

of the Greco-Roman astronomer Ptolemy (CE 90–168) and the medieval scholars who had drawn on Classical works, were at last called into question. The Aristotelian concept of four elements (earth, fire, air and water) making up all matter, and Ptolemy's model of the universe that placed the Earth at the center, are just two of the traditional beliefs that finally came to be challenged. Aristotle

St Augustine was born in Hippo Regius (present-day Algeria). He lived a famously intemperate life before his conversion in 389.

91

would doubtless have been amused that his preferred method of empirical investigation dethroned his own accounts of the physical world.

Progress was neither smooth nor easy. The Church had at its heart the belief that the world is unchanging and eternal, that man is at the center of the universe, and that the ways of God are a mystery not to be investigated. The suggestion that the Earth might not be at the center of the universe, where Ptolemy put it, was considered heretical by some religious authorities. Although in 1616 the Inquisition forced the Italian astronomer Galileo Galilei (1564–1642) to recant his belief in the Copernican theory that the Earth moves around the Sun, it could not stem the tide forever. Eventually, with the weight of scientific evidence steadily building up, the stranglehold of religious dogma weakened. Indeed, for the first time, some scientists went so far as to doubt the existence of God and put reason above faith in the hierarchy of tools for finding out about the world.

The impact on philosophy was profound. By shifting the ground under everyone's feet, the scientific revolution called into question the very nature of knowledge and certainty. Beliefs that had been held for

The Vatican put Galileo under permanent house arrest in 1633 and banned him from teaching that the Earth moves around the Sun. His book Dialogue on the Two Chief World Systems *was not removed from the index of prohibited books until 1824, and the Vatican did not apologize for its treatment of Galileo until 2000.*

Ptolemy's model of the solar system, proposed in his Almagest
*(c. CE150), put the Earth at the center of a set of concentric spheres,
the other heavenly bodies moving around it. As astronomical
observations undermined the model, it was subject to more and more
fudging to keep it a tolerable fit for observed reality.*

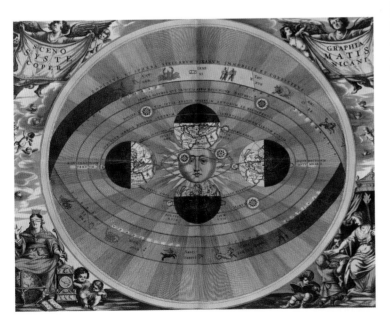

*The Polish astronomer Copernicus proposed that the Sun is at
the center of the solar system and the Earth, along with the other
planets, moves around it.*

THE EARTH MOVED FOR COPERNICUS

The Polish mathematician and astronomer Nikolaj Kopernik, better known as Nicolaus Copernicus (1473–1543), developed the heliocentric model of the solar system that put the Sun at the center with the planets revolving around it. Worried about its reception, he did not release his treatise, *On the Revolution of the Celestial Spheres*, for publication until just before his death in 1543. It did not immediately have the huge impact it was later to achieve. The Vatican added it to the list of prohibited books in 1616, 73 years after Copernicus" death, though the list had been started in 1559. Even so, his ideas were known during his lifetime and attracted criticism. The German religious reformer Philipp Melanchthon (1497–1560) said the model should be repressed by law on the grounds that "the evidence of the senses, the thousand-year consensus of men of science, and the authority of the Bible" contradicted Copernicus.

nearly two thousand years slowly became untenable. What guarantee was there that those which replaced them were ultimately any more secure?

"What do I know?"

The French Renaissance writer Michel de Montaigne was one of those who realized that the scientific revolution left no place for certainty. It appeared that reason is not a universal standard, nor are our senses reliable witnesses, so a degree of general scepticism seemed the most appropriate approach. Sometimes his scepticism seems to have left him rudderless, denied all hope of certainty or direction. "What do I know?" he asked in his essay *An Apology for Raymond Sebond* – it was to become a refrain throughout his work. He used the case of Martin Guerre as an example. The real Martin Guerre went off to war and two years later an imposter returned, claiming to be him. The man knew things only the real Guerre could have known and fooled even Guerre's wife. Montaigne argued that if a woman cannot be certain who her husband is, what can anyone be sure of?

Elsewhere, Montaigne's scepticism was liberating, as Empiricus said it should be. Being freed from false certainties gives the individual more autonomy. Montaigne saw new scientific discoveries and theories

MICHEL DE MONTAIGNE (1533–92)

Michel de Montaigne was born into a wealthy French family. He had an unusual childhood, overseen by his humanist father. It included speaking only Latin at home, three years in the care of a peasant family, and extensive exposure to music. After studying law, he worked for eleven years in regional and national courts. On his father's death in 1568, he returned to the family chateau and devoted the rest of his life to thinking and writing.

He wrote three volumes of essays, reflecting on how humans relate to each other and the world. An exceptionally eloquent humanist, Montaigne applied his great erudition to a wide range of topics. His personality shines through his writing.

Montaigne's works were not always consistent, which he would probably have regarded as a virtue. He was engaged in a sort of dialogue with himself, which continued throughout his life.

> *"That such a man wrote has truly augmented the joy of living on earth."*
>
> Friedrich Nietszche, commenting on Montaigne

as contributing to an endless process of discovery – not as something that should be accepted immediately as unchallenged truth, but as steps towards what might or might not be accurate. He believed that knowledge could as easily stifle enquiry as promote it, if it were accepted uncritically. It was most important, he considered, to keep challenging and reviewing our opinions, continuing with critical enquiry, and conducting an ongoing reappraisal of the way that we live.

Despite his scepticism, Montaigne was a practising Catholic. He saw no contradiction in this. On the contrary, he claimed that scepticism in non-religious matters made it easier to accept religious truths, which can only be justified through faith.

Towards science

While Montaigne was first and foremost a thinker, the English philosopher Francis Bacon (1561–1626) was at the heart of the scientific revolution and his most notable work was on developing the scientific method.

Bacon took issue with both the Platonic and Aristotelian approaches to knowledge. Bacon considered rationalism, which approached knowledge through reason and by examining the meaning of words, to be the equivalent of spinning a web from the inside of one's own head. He thought Aristotelian empiricism was little better; the empirical approach involved amassing data, but that

Francis Bacon initiated the scientific method, demanding a proper investigation of any hypothesis.

did not in itself yield any useful ideas. Bacon insisted that better ways of collating and organizing data would help to generate inductive hypotheses that could then be tested by scientific means.

Bacon realized that instead of trying to show that something will always happen, there is more mileage in disproving hypotheses. This seems counterintuitive, as it suggests that science can progress most quickly by being wrong. But it does makes sense. If we toss a coin a million times and it comes down heads each time, we still can't say it will always come down heads. But if it once comes down tails, we can dismiss the hypothesis that it will always come down heads. This bears a striking resemblance to the "falsificationist" scientific methodology developed by 20th-century philosopher Karl Popper. In his claim to have solved the problem of induction, Popper openly acknowledged his debt to Bacon.

Francis Bacon was not primarily interested in the problem of induction, though. He was more concerned with method, and in particular with finding a method to generate good inductive hypotheses from the data that scientists were gathering.

He devised a new method, which he illustrated by suggesting an investigation into the nature of heat. He said we should first list all things in which heat is present,

> ## THE PROBLEM OF INDUCTION
> The so-called problem of induction taxed many thinkers of the scientific revolution. In essence, it is a problem of drawing conclusions from a mass of data. If you toss a coin twenty times and it comes down heads every time, it might be tempting to suppose that it is more likely to come down tails the next time, but this is not true. The chance of heads or tails remains the same for the first throw, the twenty-first throw, and for the thousand and first throw. The preceding events have no impact on the future event, and we can't induce anything from the mass of preceding throws of the coin. Simple repetition does not guarantee anything, though it can lead us to draw up a hypothesis. So, seeing that the Sun has risen in the east every day in recorded history, we might hypothesize that it will always rise in the east. But we should need something other than previous observations to convince us that that will be the case.

then all things in which it is absent and finally all those that can be of varying temperature. Bacon believed that a natural hypothesis would present itself from the list. His list of hot things begins:

1. The rays of the Sun, particularly in summer, and at noon.
2. The same reflected and condensed, as between mountains, or along walls, and particularly in burning mirrors.
3. Ignited meteors.
4. Burning lightning
5. Eruptions of flames from the cavities of mountains, etc.
6. Flame of every kind.
7. Ignited solids.
8. Natural warm water baths.

Bacon included the lava that erupts from volcanoes in his list of hot things.

Bacon concluded that movement is the source of heat, and that hot things are characterized by movement outwards and upwards. Often, it is not the whole body that moves, but the particles that make it up – so boiling water seethes in the pot and flames dance around.

Sadly, Bacon's investigations around heat were eventually to be his downfall – he died of pneumonia while experimenting with a method for freezing chicken. But it seems unlikely that Bacon's method would often generate useful hypotheses, or that there could ever be a single way of organizing data that would make hypotheses become immediately apparent. It will always take creativity and imagination to see the patterns and potential in a body of data, and so to begin building theories to account for them. Even so, Bacon is credited with the invention of the scientific method, and was instrumental in making science of practical benefit to mankind, using it to produce "inventions, which shall overcome, to some extent, and subdue our needs and

KNOWLEDGE IS POWER – IN THE WRONG HANDS

The French social theorist Michel Foucault (1926–84) was the first postmodernist philosopher. The relationship between power and knowledge, and how power is used to control and define knowledge, runs through all of Foucault's work. He saw scientific knowledge not as a means of empowering ordinary people, but as a means of social control. During the 18th century, for example, the label of "madness" – the opposite of "reason" – was used to stigmatize all kinds of socially undesirable people. These included the poor, the homeless and anyone else considered a social nuisance, not just those with genuine mental illness. He considered the emergence of prison sentences to replace public executions as another demonstration of power, an extended and dehumanizing punishment being more of a deterrent and a more effective show of power than a quick execution.

With Freud's psychoanalysis, the new concentration on sexuality as an aspect of psychology provided another way of controlling people. If sexual intentions and preferences are considered to give an insight into personality, people become wary of revealing too much about themselves at the same time as they are encouraged to be more open about their sexuality. All these aspects of knowledge and identity change through time, but they don't vary along a path of linear progress. Instead, they change as those in power use them to their own ends to control the behavior of others.

Foucault maintained that this dismal state of affairs could be countered by using philosophy to redress the power balance. Once we have recognized how those in power try to control us, we can prevent it and re-examine our knowledge in the light of what he has said about how knowledge is socially constructed as a tool of manipulation and control.

miseries". Bacon is sometimes considered to be the philosophical inspiration behind the Industrial Revolution and has been credited with first saying "knowledge is power" (though the phrase does not appear in his writings).

Thinking and being

René Descartes" most famous philosophical work is *Meditations on First Philosophy* (1641), known simply as *Meditations*, in which he set out to establish the foundations of knowledge. His own work extended far

> *"If I chance to look out of the window onto men passing in the street, I do not fail to say, on seeing them, that I see men . . . and yet, what do I see from this window, other than hats and cloaks, which cover ghosts or dummies who move only by means of springs? But I judge them to be really men, and thus I understand, by the sole power of judgement that resides in my mind, what I believed I saw with my eyes."*
>
> René Descartes,
> *Meditations* (1641)

beyond philosophy to encompass various aspects of physics, including optics, and mathematics; he developed the system of Cartesian coordinates used for plotting graphs by mapping points on x, y and z axes.

In his *Meditations*, Descartes began by examining his own beliefs to decide which he felt were secure. He decided that some were easier to justify than others, with some appearing certain – such as mathematical "truths" – and some having shakier foundations or even being revealed as false on closer inspection. He decided that he needed to be able to justify each proposition by grounding it in a secure belief, but this left him with the question of where he could start – what is the infallible first proposition? Instead of trying to put all his beliefs in order, showing which followed from each, he tested each by asking, what was its source? If the source was infallible, he could consider the belief secure. If the source was not infallible, no knowledge based on that source could be considered reliable.

Descartes recognized that many of his beliefs were based on evidence from his senses: from what he could see, hear or feel. But our senses are not entirely reliable: a stick appears to be bent when placed in a glass of water, for example. Descartes then proposed that at least he could be sure that he was a Frenchman interested in philosophy who was sitting in his study, and so on. But then there is no clear way of distinguishing between reality and dreaming. How does he know that the life he thinks he is leading is not just part of a dream? Hallucinations can even make us believe in something that is not there at all, with our senses deceiving us entirely. All knowledge rooted in sensory perception is therefore suspect.

Turning to his own reason, Descartes tests his knowledge that 2 + 3 = 5, that a mother is older than her daughter, and that a triangle has three sides. These beliefs look secure, but could be the result of a massive deception. He imagines the possibility of a supremely powerful, but malign, demon who could manipulate his thoughts and instil these false beliefs.

There is, though, one proposition that even a supremely powerful being could not manipulate and this is that Descartes exists because he is thinking (even though what he is thinking may be false). He must exist in order to think. Hence Descartes arrived at his famous maxim *cogito ergo sum* – "I think therefore I am". The *cogito*, as it is known, was his one solid, infallible foundation of knowledge.

Descartes intended to begin from the *cogito* and his certain knowledge that God exists, and so guarantee the security of

In the film The Matrix *(1999), what most people perceive as reality is in fact an illusion created by the evil artificial intelligence that runs the world – similar to the "evil demon" that Descartes says could be deceiving us into believing "reality" exists.*

his knowledge. But later philosophers found his subsequent arguments in the *Meditations* unconvincing, and it has instead come to be viewed as the primary text on epistemological scepticism.

Reason and experience in the Age of Reason

Descartes was a scientist as well as a philosopher, and was writing at the start of the scientific and philosophical revolution that came to be known as the "Age of Reason". Bacon and Descartes were the earliest modern philosophers in the traditions of empiricism and rationalism that we can trace back to Plato and Aristotle. It was the German philosopher Immanuel Kant (1724–1804) who named these two strands of philosophy. Following Descartes in the rationalist camp were Baruch Spinoza and Gottfried Leibniz, while the English philosophers Thomas Hobbes (1588–1679) and John Locke built on the earlier work of Bacon.

Locke was profoundly influenced by the scientific work of his contemporaries the English mathematician Isaac Newton (*see* panel opposite) and the Irish chemist

Robert Boyle (1627–91). Locke set out to explain human understanding in a way consistent with Newtonian mechanics, putting epistemology on a scientific footing.

He spent twenty years writing his *Essay Concerning Human Understanding* (1690), which was to exert a huge influence over the development of Western philosophy over the next hundred years.

Locke set out to investigate how the human mind collects, organizes and classifies data and makes judgements based on it – in his own words, "to inquire into the original, certainty and extent of human knowledge". He rejected the rationalist philosophy of Descartes, believing that knowledge must come from experience, through the actions of the physical world on our senses.

He introduced the idea of the mind of the newborn as a *tabula rasa*, or blank slate. The infant knows nothing, has no innate

Is a baby born with a completely empty mind? Locke said that it was; Kant said it must have some knowledge in order to be able to interpret sensory perceptions and build knowledge from them.

ISAAC NEWTON (1642–1727)

The English mathematician and physicist Isaac Newton made ground-breaking discoveries in mathematics and physics that underpinned the scientific revolution. He demonstrated that the universe runs according to predictable physical and mechanical laws. Newton's statement of the law of universal gravitation, from which he was able to explain and predict the movement of the Moon and planets, was not challenged until the work of Albert Einstein in the early 20th century. Newton's methods were empirical and inductive, and he criticized Descartes" rationalist, deductive approach to knowledge.

George Berkeley (1685–1753) was Bishop of Cloyne in the south of Ireland. He believed our senses could not give us reliable information about the nature of reality and that things "out there" don't really exist.

no synthesis by the mind. Complex ideas are constructed in the mind from simple ideas and require some mental operation. So, recognizing a dog or a table from the collection of sensory data we receive from these objects involves thought – a dog or a table is a complex idea. Complex ideas need not relate to things that actually exist, hence we can conceive of a unicorn, which does not exist but is made up of two other complex ideas, "horse" and "horn".

Simple ideas are divided into primary and secondary qualities of objects. Primary qualities are those that Locke considered to be inherent and essential to all objects, such as solidity, extension in space, shape, motion or rest, and number. Secondary qualities are those that are apparent because of our sensory perception of them, such as color, scent and taste. They are not inherent in the objects, but produced in our minds when we become aware of the objects. Primary qualities can be thought of as objective (they really exist, independent of an observer), and secondary qualities as subjective, depending on the presence of an observer to exist. In Locke's schema, there is no such thing as color or sound without a perceiving mind. This view is shared by some modern philosophers and scientists.

knowledge, and all that he or she learns is derived from the world of experience. The direct product of stimulation of the senses is simple ideas, such as "hot", "cold", "round", "hard", "sweet", "yellow" and so on. These are things that we can experience directly and require

---

SPOTLIGHT ON PHILOSOPHERS

Does a tree falling over in the forest make a sound if there is no one to hear it?

Locke: No. It produces vibrations in the air, but sound is a secondary quality that exists only in the mind of the observer.

Berkeley: No. And there wasn't a tree in the first place.

Now you see it, now you don't

George Berkeley is regarded as the father of philosophical idealism, which attempted to show that the materialist view of Locke and Newton was untenable.

Berkeley was not alone in seeing that Locke's causal theory of perception implied there is a logical gap between the subject (the perceiving mind) and reality. (This gap is sometimes called "the veil of perception".)

"The objects of sense exist only when they are perceived; the trees therefore are in the garden . . . no longer than while there is somebody by to perceive them." George Berkeley, A Treatise Concerning the Principles of Human Knowledge *(1710)*

SCIENTIFIC ESSENTIALISM

The American philosophers Saul Kripke (born 1940) and Hilary Putnam (born 1926) propose a modern scheme comparable with Locke's view of essential properties. This states that all objects have essential properties that they necessarily possess if they are to be identified as a specific type of object. For example, all tigers must possess tiger DNA. Other properties, such as having striped fur and four legs, are not essential – a tiger would remain a tiger if it were an albino with no stripes or had lost a leg. The essential properties are necessary *but not sufficient* to define the object in its class – so a tiger steak has tiger DNA, but is not in itself a tiger.

When we see something, it is as a result of objects in the external world having a physical, causal effect on our senses and so producing an idea in our mind. If you look at a cat, light reflected from the cat and falling on the retina of your eye causes a signal to travel along neural pathways from the retina to the brain with the result that you "see" a cat. The image of the cat is constructed in your brain and is no guarantee of the real existence of the cat, or that it "really" looks the way you see it. (You could dream of a cat, or see one in a hallucination, without any real cat being present.)

Berkeley called the perception of the cat the "idea" of the cat. It might be that cats in reality are altogether different from how we see them – we have no way of telling. Locke had backed away from this bold conclusion by distinguishing between primary qualities

> *"To be is to be perceived."*
>
> George Berkeley

Until 1869, pandas were considered mythical. **Not** *seeing something is no guarantee that it* **doesn't** *exist.*

see it, it isn't there. This is problematic, as our general belief is that things continue to exist even when we are not looking at them. If you go out of the bathroom and close the door (leaving no one else inside), do the contents of the bathroom cease to exist? Do they wink in and out of existence as you open and close the door? Berkeley had an answer to this: our perceptions are produced for us by God, and as God is all-seeing, things continue to be perceived by Him even when we are not looking. God keeps the bathroom in existence when you are no longer in it.

Perception is all, God is nil

The Scottish philosopher David Hume followed in the footsteps of Locke, claiming that only knowledge that can be gained through our senses is valid and anything else is simply invention and must be rejected. As

that really exist in an object and secondary qualities that exist only in the mind of the beholder. Berkeley saw no such distinction, and so left reality without a leg to stand on.

Clearly, following this line of argument, if something is not an idea in someone's mind, it doesn't exist. If you don't see the cat, who is to say it's there? In fact, if you don't

> *There was a young man who said, "God*
> *Must think it exceedingly odd*
> *If he finds that this tree*
> *Continues to be*
> *When there's no one about in the Quad."*
> *Reply:*
> *Dear Sir:*
> *Your astonishment's odd:*
> *I am always about in the Quad.*
> *And that's why the tree*
> *Will continue to be,*
> *Since observed by*
> *Yours faithfully,*
> *GOD.*
>
> Ronald Knox, theologian (1888–1957)

QUANTUM THEORY AND OBSERVATION

In quantum physics, the role of the observer in the existence of phenomena seems to find scientific confirmation. The famous double-slit experiment and its variants examine the wave/particle properties of light (and, in later versions, of electrons and even molecules). The outcome of the experiment is altered by introducing equipment to observe what is happening – in some cases, the behavior of a particle/wave is apparently even altered retrospectively. The physics is too complex to explain here, but the philosophical impact of these findings is far-reaching. It really is impossible to know anything if what is true is determined by the observing of it.

On the one hand, this seems fair: we see that one event is regularly followed by another, but that is not evidence that one causes the other. We have simply interpreted one as cause and the other as effect. It is easy to infer causation incorrectly: in the summer, sales of barbecues go up and more people go to the beach, but one does not cause the other; there is a different cause (improving

a consequence, he had to deny the existence of God, of the self, all causation and even the validity of inductive knowledge (that derived through reasoning). Hume's scepticism was reductive in the extreme.

Observing that we can never experience our own self, only a chain of experiences, he concluded that the self is an illusion. "I am nothing but a bundle of perceptions," he wrote, meaning that human identity is only the sum of a stream of sense-experiences. Similarly, we don't experience or perceive the mechanism by which one event necessarily follows another (causation), we only experience the sequence of events. As we have no means of experiencing causation, Hume rejected it as illusory.

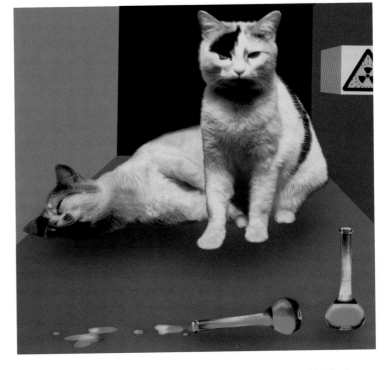

In Erwin Schrödinger's thought experiment devised in 1935, the condition of a cat – dead or alive – is not fixed in a single state until an observer looks at it. At that point, quantum possibilities collapse and the cat ceases to be both dead and alive at the same time and becomes either dead or alive.

David Hume was the most extreme of sceptics, being unwilling to accept any knowledge not perceived directly by the senses.

weather) behind both trends. On the other hand, Hume's view doesn't allow what we would consider to be obvious and genuine causation to be acknowledged. If you throw a stone at a window, and the window breaks, you can't – according to Hume – infer that the impact of the stone on the window causes the window to break.

Hume's intention was both to rid science of all falsehoods ("inventions" not based in experience) and to establish a new science of human nature. In his *Treatise on Human Nature* (1739–40) he set out to find general principles or rules in psychology that would allow him to produce a mechanized view of understanding comparable to Newton's

mechanized view of the physical universe. His categorization of impressions and ideas, though, owed much to Descartes, whose work he rejected. This meant that Hume failed in his goal of creating a replacement science, but succeeded in his first ambition of removing "falsehoods". Indeed, his critique of inductive reasoning was devastating, and colored philosophy for the next two centuries.

Inductive reasoning is at the heart of all scientific endeavour: we infer scientific laws by looking at the world and searching for explanations that account for what we can see happening. Hume says that this is not a valid way to proceed, and that we are not justified in assuming that there are not instances we haven't observed that would disprove the "rule". The best response to the problem of induction comes from Karl Popper who pointed out that we can draw inferences from negative discoveries (falsification of hypotheses). So if we see 100 brown lions and one grey lion, we can infer that not all lions are brown.

From empiricism to positivism

Much later, the Austrian philosopher of science Ernst Mach (1838–1916) took an empiricist view that recalls Hume's extreme scepticism. He declared that: "We know only one source which directly reveals scientific facts – our senses." No metaphysical contemplation carried any validity. In Mach's view, science should be reconstructed as an account of the facts that can be extracted from our sensory experience of the world. Anything that strays outside the description of sensory experience is stepping beyond the evidence available to us and so cannot be justified. The laws of nature that we seem to discover are, he said, simply the product of our minds wishing to impose order on our surroundings. In different cultures, places and times, different sets of explanations have been deemed suitable.

If the laws of nature are not laws at all, there is no way in which they can really be "proved" as there is no objective truth behind them. The validity of any law of science can be measured only insofar as it helpfully explains and structures the world for us, so that we feel content and secure and are best able to control and predict our environment. This leads to a pragmatic approach to scientific theorizing. If there is more than one possible way of explaining

> *"According to our conception, natural laws are a product of our psychological need to feel at home with nature; all concepts transcending sensation are to be justified as helping us to understand, control and predict our environment, and different conceptual systems may be used to this end in different cultures and at different times with equal propriety."*
>
> Ernst Mach

something, but none has the benefit of absolute truth, how are we to choose between them? Mach suggests applying principles of simplicity, consistency and depth. Although there might be no absolute value in simplicity (*see* panel on page 108), it has often been thought a useful measure in choosing between scientific theories. Consistency means that there should not be contradictions in the scheme, and depth means that it should have great explanatory force.

There is a problem with Mach's view of science. Anything that we can't actually observe is, to all intents and purposes, non-existent. This includes atoms, black holes, the early geological history of

Ernst Mach took an approach that would later be called positivism, relying entirely on observable phenomena and saying that we construct "laws" of physics and nature to help us codify reality as we experience it.

the planet, tectonic plates, magnetism, waves, gravity, time and space. Mach even said that to afford such things any material status was to invoke "the sham ideas of the old metaphysics". The American Willard Quine (1908–2000) made a similar point when he said that the posits of theoretical physics have no better epistemological basis than Homer's gods.

Mach's determination to rely wholly on sense-data means that he seems either to deny the existence of things we can't perceive, or deny that we can ever have knowledge of those things. In the second case, he would be aligning himself with Kant and his view of the unknowable "noumenal world", as he called it.

OCCAM'S RAZOR

The principle known as Occam's razor has been stated in different forms by several philosophers. The central idea is that if there are two possible explanations, equally attractive in other regards, the simpler is to be preferred. In fact, there is no sound epistemological reason for assuming a simple explanation is more likely to be correct than a more complex one.

Mediating between reason and experience

The divide between the empiricists on the one hand and the rationalists on the other had brought philosophy to something of an impasse in the 18th century. Over the following 200 years, there would be attempts to bridge the gap or reject both approaches in favour of an attempt at something new.

Immanuel Kant believed that the concepts of space and time, of cause and effect, were programmed into the human brain and colored our perception of all experiences – even dinner with friends.

Constructing knowledge

Immanuel Kant tried to solve the problem by bridging the gap, showing that both approaches had some merit. In his *Critique of Pure Reason* (1781) he set out to explain how we can make objective judgements about reality. Then, in his *Critique of Practical Reason* (1788), he tried to justify ethical judgements by applying reason.

Kant began his task of reconciling reason and experience by asking, "what are the necessary preconditions for having any experience at all?" He then suggested that we can only make any sense of our experiences – the data gathered by our senses – if we have structures for interpreting them. The new, untutored mind of

This self-portrait of NASA's Mars rover Curiosity combines dozens of exposures taken by the rover's imager during one Martian day, or sol. Curiosity applies algorithms to incoming data from sensors to provide "knowledge" about the surrounding environment. In the same way, Kant would argue, the human brain applies structures to incoming sense-data to enable us to interpret experience.

the newborn is not entirely a *tabula rasa* as Locke said it was, because if the infant did not have ways of making sense of what it sees and hears it could never construct any knowledge.

Kant argued that the mind imposes structures on the incoming data. He proposed twelve fundamental judgements, or Categories: substance, cause/effect, reciprocity, necessity, possibility, existence, totality, unity, plurality, limitation, reality and negation. These Categories must be applied within the structures of space and time, which he called "forms of intuition". By applying Categories, with reference to the place and time the data were received, the mind can make sense of the world. Kant was so proud of this idea that he referred to it as his "Copernican revolution", believing that it overturned the previous world-order and finally explained how the mind generates knowledge by imposing principles on experience.

But there was a problem with Kant's approach. If the human mind could only apply structures to the data gathered by the senses, that left the reason under-employed and the realm of metaphysics untouched. The rationalists (such as Descartes) constructed knowledge purely from within the mind, and could deal with abstract concepts such as justice, beauty, the self and virtue. Kant's construction of knowledge required sense-data as the starting point for everything, so had no space for anything that doesn't begin with experience. Our knowledge can only be a systematization of experience – it can't extend to the reality behind what we perceive, the noumenal world (*see* panel below).

The path to truth

Although Kant considered the gap between the noumenal and the phenomenal worlds (the real and perceived) to be unavoidable, Hegel found it unacceptable and wanted to close it.

Hegel believed there was an ultimate truth, and it was accessible to human understanding. The path to discovery lay in a process called "dialectic", and it is a process that takes place over the whole, slowly unfolding history of human thought. Hegelian dialectic begins with a notion, or thesis, that is deemed to be true. If we reflect on this thesis, we discover that there is another possible point of view that contradicts it. This is called the "antithesis". Comparison and consideration of these opposing points of view often reveal a third way that might be something of a compromise, or a middle path. This is called the "synthesis". The synthesis becomes the new thesis and then a new antithesis emerges to contradict it, and so a new synthesis must be found, and so on. Through a process of iteration, we creep closer to truth.

But it is not a truth in the sense that one proposition is true and another is not. For Hegel, truth was not propositional – instead, it was conceptual, and to do with completeness. The progression towards truth is really a progression towards a universal mind or spirit. In Hegel's scheme, a scientific theory that has been shown

THE NOUMENAL AND PHENOMENAL WORLDS

According to Kant, the world we experience is the phenomenal world: it is in this that we see landscapes, hear birds sing, eat food and drink wine. Our minds make sense of the data our brains receive through these experiences. What lies beyond these instances of reality that impinge on us is the noumenal world, "the thing-in-itself" (*das Ding an sich*), which is not accessible to human knowledge. If we viewed everything through a distorting glass for our whole lives, we would see everything differently but be unaware that our perception was distorted. Similarly, we can't know how the perceived world (the phenomenal world) relates to the real state of the world (the noumenal world).

> *"The significance of that "absolute" commandment, "know thyself",*
> *whether we look at it in itself or under the historical circumstance of*
> *its first utterance – is not to promote mere self-knowledge in respect*
> *of the particular capacities . . . of the single self. The knowledge*
> *it commands means that of man's genuine reality – of what is*
> *essentially and ultimately true and real – of spirit as the true and*
> *essential being."*
>
> George Hegel

to be wrong or inadequate is merely incomplete. The Newtonian laws of gravitation were accepted as wholly correct for many centuries, but Einstein showed that they don't apply to very small bodies (such as atoms) and perhaps not to bodies larger than galaxies. This didn't make the law of gravitation wrong – it just meant it was limited, an incomplete understanding of the absolute truth. Attaining absolute truth means overcoming all limitations. It ends with a grand metaphysical concept of a universal mind.

George Hegel proposed a way of approaching truth through a series of theses that build on each other over time, a more complete one always replacing a less complete one.

Arthur Schopenhauer was a contemporary of Hegel. Although he disliked Hegel, Schopenhauer also took as his starting point the unknowability of things-in-themselves, the "real" reality behind the phenomenal world as described by Kant. But Schopenhauer posited a sort of sneaky back door by which we *can* know things-in-themselves. We have to realize that "we ourselves are among those entities we want to know, so we too are a thing-in-itself." He meant that the subjective "I" is only revealed to us in the world of phenomena, so it can't constitute our real essence (the "thing-in-itself"). Our real essence is will, the universal striving force manifest, trapped, in each individual being by its insatiable desire to reveal itself in the world of appearances. Recognizing the will lets us know the "thing-in-itself" that is the "I".

Phenomenalism is essentially subjective: it says that all we have to work with is how we experience the world rather than what the world really is.

There are different levels of phenomenalism. Kant can be called an epistemological phenomenalist, as he believed that all we can know is the act of experiencing. George Berkeley can be called an ontological phenomenalist, as he believed that all that exists is the act of experiencing.

The rise of phenomenalism

The German mathematician and philosopher Edmund Husserl (1859–1938) saw science not as an empirical enterprise but as principally rational. Like Descartes, he thought philosophy must begin with the self-evidence of the individual's subjectivity. Science, in Husserl's view, is an exploration of perception, belief, judgement and other mental processes rather than of the world "out there". This position – that we can only deal with the sense-impressions made on us by phenomena, and cannot deal directly with whatever "reality" causes those impressions – is called *phenomenalism*. It is central to existentialism and, after Husserl, was explored by Heidegger, Merleau-Ponty and Sartre.

Husserl began with the concept of "intentionality", which he took from German psychologist Franz Brentano (1838–1917). According to Brentano, all mental acts are directed towards an object. If we think of the city of Paris, the thought is directed towards the object, Paris. If we rage against injustice, our anger is directed towards injustice (the object can be abstract in nature). If we fear ghosts, the fear is directed towards ghosts (the object need not exist in reality – the fear exists whether or not ghosts exist). Husserl suggested that the intentionality of the mind entails that the conscious state (thought, rage, fear) can't be separated from its object (Paris, injustice, ghosts). They exist together, as two aspects of one phenomenon, the intentional act.

So Husserl saw consciousness as "directedness towards an object" (whether or not there is a physical external object). The aim of philosophy, he believed, is to understand how this directedness manifests

Arthur Schopenhauer saw all of creation driven by a universal Will, a striving force desperate to be realized and recognized.

For Edmund Husserl any reality that might correspond to the city of Paris is less important to us than the act of seeing or contemplating the city of Paris.

itself. He considered this a non-empirical version of science: one that investigates only the subjective elements of the mental processes of experience.

Husserl's investigation didn't need to pay any heed to what, if anything, "out there" lies behind the mental act. He was interested only in what he could consider certainties, and they lay within the conscious mind and the acts of consciousness. Like Descartes, Husserl realized that he could not say anything certain about the world "out there", outside the mind. That did not greatly bother him; what did bother him was that he was faced with a sceptical position regarding consciousness, or "knowledge of self". By his own definition, consciousness is identified with the intentional act, but it is not the act, it is observing the act. The self (or consciousness) can't be the object of an intentional act because it can't be both observed and observer. He was led to conclude that the subject of experience (the self) is transcendental – inhabiting some other realm. This was a return to Descartes'' dualist position in which the self and the external world (and by extension, the mind and the body) occupy distinct realms.

The French philosopher Maurice Merleau-Ponty (1908–61) was greatly influenced by Husserl and also adopted a phenomenological approach, focusing on the embodied experience without reference to the objective reality (or otherwise) of the world experienced.

Merleau-Ponty found both empiricism and rationalism unsatisfactory, partly because they both fail to answer Meno's paradox: that you can't look for something you don't know as you won't recognize it if you find it.

Empiricists look at the world as something separate from the mind – the conscious mind is the subject and the world is the object. We experience the world in a rich, multi-layered way, and always in a complex context. But to make sense of it, we try to order it, breaking this continuum of experience into discrete chunks. We can't know whether the way we put these chunks together in our minds is an accurate representation of the reality (assuming there is an objectively real world). This means that the external world remains unknowable, and Meno's paradox stands. Rationalism (which Merleau-Ponty calls intellectualism) also falls foul of Meno's paradox: if knowledge exists *a priori*, then why bother searching for it?

Merleau-Ponty put perception in pride of place in his scheme. He couldn't reconcile rationalism with his view, since it gave no importance to perception in the process of acquiring knowledge, and took no real notice of the body and the reality of our existence as embodied beings. He couldn't accept empiricism as it breaks down sense-perceptions in an atomistic way that does not relate to reality as we experience it. Instead, he saw perception as experienced through the "lived body". By this, he meant that the subject (consciousness) is not something that exists only in the mind, but is experienced in and through the whole body. He rejected Descartes" view of the body as a physiological mechanism inhabited by a separate and "other" spirit. Merleau-Ponty saw the body and mind as an integrated mechanism; the mind is not just an inhabitant, and the act of perception is not just the impact of sense-data on sensory organs but something that involves the intellect.

We derive meaning from our experiences through the way we perceive them in relation to our bodies – hot or cold, big or small, near or far. Our experience of spatial location depends on how our own bodies occupy space and a specific location. Our experience of time is dictated by our inability to inhabit any moment but the present, so defining our sense of the past and future.

Describing experience as a subject-object dialogue, Merleau-Ponty reminded

EMPIRICISTS

"Empiricism cannot see that we need to know what we are looking for, otherwise we would not be looking for it, and intellectualism fails to see that we need to be ignorant of what we are looking for, or equally again we should not be searching."

Maurice Merleau-Ponty, *The Phenomenology of Perception* (1945)

A. J. Ayer was a good tap-dancer and once said he would rather have been a tap-dancer than a philosopher. He gave up the ambition when he realized that he would never be as good as Fred Astaire.

us that each experience is perceived with everything that surrounds it in space and everything that has preceded it in time. He broke out of the mind/world dualism and put the body in a third state between them. He resolved Meno's paradox, too. How do we know that we have found what we are looking for if we do not yet know what it is? Because the embodied experience gives it meaning. At first, our perceptions are fuzzy and ambiguous, but as we become more bodily engaged with the world, things become more defined and certain.

Looking sideways at reality

Empiricism flourished in the 20th century, perhaps encouraged or supported by rapid advances in science and the increasing interest that philosophers took in the basis of scientific knowledge. The British philosopher Alfred Ayer (1910–89), better known as A. J. Ayer, was an empiricist in the tradition of Hume. He developed a robust form of empiricism that he called "linguistic phenomenalism". Generally, phenomenalism considers objects in the material world to be constructions in the mind made from sense-data. In Ayer's version, statements about material objects can really only be statements about the sense-data we receive, as the objects are not observable or knowable.

Ayer maintained that any statement about material objects can be reduced to statements about sense-data. So if we see a tree in a garden, all we can really say is that if we go to a place that is known as the garden we will experience sense-data about (that is, see) something that exhibits "tree-ness". And the reason we will see something that exhibits tree-ness is because that is what happens if you go into that garden (not necessarily because there is a tree – or anything else that exhibits tree-ness). Although Ayer was attempting to be more rigorous in what we can be certain about, he ended up with something that is rather vague and uncertain.

Logical positivism

Ayer is perhaps best remembered for setting out the stall of *logical positivism*, a strand in 20th-century thinking that severely limited the scope of philosophy. According to logical positivists, philosophy is concerned with organizing thoughts. "True" statements fall into two categories. They are either "tautologies", which are the truths of mathematics and logic and just "are" true, or they are the verifiable empirical claims of science. Any other type of statement, including anything about metaphysics or religion, is simply meaningless – it's not even untrue. The logical positivists depend on the principle of verificationism: the validity of a statement rests on its ability either to be verified from experience or by virtue of its being "analytic" – demonstrable by logic starting from a statement that is accepted as true. Beginning before the outbreak of World War II, logical positivism arose from the so-called Vienna Circle and Berlin Circle, groups of philosophers sharing ideas in – unsurprisingly – Vienna and Berlin.

Verifying and falsifying

The philosopher Karl Popper responded to verificationism with the method he called

$$PS_1 \longrightarrow TT \longrightarrow EE \longrightarrow PS_2$$

A problem situation (PS_1) gives rise to some tentative theories (TT). An iterative process of error elimination (EE) leads to a better understanding and the statement of a more complex or interesting problem situation (PS_2).

"falsificationism" – a method that he claimed solved Hume's problem of induction. Hume believed that by examining collected data we can see patterns that lead us to theories or to extracting rules. The difficulty is that we can never examine all possible examples. So we might decide, on the basis of observation, that all foxes are red, or all swans are white. But we haven't seen every fox and every swan. People believed that all

Karl Popper (left) is considered one of the greatest philosophers of science of the 20th century.

"For my part I . . . believe in physical objects and not in Homer's gods; and I consider it a scientific error to believe otherwise. But in point of epistemological footing, the physical objects and the gods differ only in degree and not in kind. Both sorts of entities enter our conceptions only as cultural posits."

Willard Quine,
Two Dogmas of Empiricism (1951)

swans were white until black swans were seen. There is nothing to say we won't one day find a green fox. These conclusions drawn from observation (induced) are not robust, as a single counter-example can overturn them. Popper pointed out that it's easier to disprove a theory than to verify it.

He said that a generalization is not valid as a conclusion drawn from evidence, but has the logical status of a conjecture. It can be tested by observations that will either refute it (if we see a green fox, for instance) or it waits to be tested by further observations. Only if we had seen all foxes that have ever existed or will ever exist could the generalization that all foxes are red become a conclusion.

The mark of a scientific theory is that it can be falsified. Popper rejected psychoanalysis as a science on the grounds that its theories cannot be falsified. He saw the accumulation of scientific knowledge over time as a result of repeated falsification. As one theory after another is shown to be wrong, the stock of remaining theories (or replacement theories) is slowly whittled away, leaving those that are correct.

Willard Quine (1908–2000) was an empiricist *par excellence*. He maintained that science is "the final arbiter of truth" and only science can tell us about the world. Even so, our knowledge of the world is limited by our reception and interpretation of sense-data. In *Two Dogmas of Empiricism* (1951), he took up two stands against established positivist positions. First, he attacked Kant's distinction between analytic propositions, which are by definition true (such as "all corpses are dead"), and synthetic propositions, which are true or false according to circumstance (that it is raining, for instance). Secondly, he rejected the claim that a statement about the material world can be reduced to statements about sense-data.

Quine argued that all propositions are tied in with sensory experience and with the "web of beliefs" in which we are embedded. We can't dissociate our experiences from the world-view we hold, so that theory and experience necessarily go hand in

PHILOSOPHERSPEAK:
ANALYTIC AND SYNTHETIC STATEMENTS
Analytic statements are true by definition – such as, "all bachelors are unmarried".
Synthetic statements have a specific subject and predicate – such as, "that bachelor is 25 years old".

Lots of people say they have seen UFOs. Some even claim to have been inside one. Yet conventional opinion is that these people are mistaken.

hand. Science is essentially a pragmatic exercise that fits experience to what we can know and predicts future experience in the light of past experience. Quine accepted that ontology (which is concerned with what exists) is relative to any particular society's beliefs.

Fighting back

The Austrian-born philosopher Paul Feyerabend (1924–94) rejected both logical positivism and Popper's falsificationism. He became famous in the 1960s and 1970s for establishing "epistemological anarchism", which attacked the assumption that science is rooted in a rational methodology.

Feyerabend began with an idea proposed by Thomas Kuhn (1922–96) that science oscillates between periods of "normal science" and "revolutionary science". According to Kuhn, there are long periods during which science pootles along, with only findings that endorse the current paradigm being given serious consideration. Then there are occasional periods of revolutionary science when everything is up for grabs and major paradigm-shifts happen. Feyerabend denied this, saying that there are always incompatible scientific theories vying for attention and it is competition that makes scientific endeavour fruitful. Even if a theory is thought adequate, suggesting alternatives is good as the challenge forces us to examine

> *"There is only one principle that can be defended under all circumstances and in all stages of human development. It is the principle: anything goes."*
> Paul Feyerabend, *Against Method* (1975)

how robust the theory really is and to test it further. He called this "theoretical pluralism". It led him towards "relativism" and "anti-realism". He rejected the usual wisdom that a theory is good if it "fits the facts" as he didn't accept that there were facts to be fitted. Feyerabend considered that all statements of fact are bound up with the beliefs and conventions that attach to the words in which they are couched. Here he draws on the "language-game" idea of Ludwig Wittgenstein, which says that all use of language is limited by social context.

Feyerabend argued that factual statements don't reflect some independent reality but are determined by social conventions and the connotations of words, and that these in turn reflect a prevailing view of the world. He suggests that instead of comparing a theory with "facts" we should compare competing theories with each other and choose the one that adds most to our understanding.

Feyerabend's doctrine of epistemological anarchism said there are no rules or methods in science that will reliably produce good results, so science is essentially anarchic. Most academics paid little regard to this extreme position, but Feyerabend enjoyed popularity among some alternative groups resisting the dogma of science.

Paul Feyerabend alienated some other philosophers with his view that no theory or factual statement actually reflects a real state of affairs.

> *"To say of what is that it is not, or of what is not that it is, is false, while to say of what is that it is, and of what is not that it is not, is true."*
>
> Aristotle, *Metaphysics*

What is truth?

We have discussed at length how philosophers consider we arrive at knowledge, at what we can consider "true", but we have said very little about what truth is. The working definition of knowledge is "a true belief", rooted in Plato's assertion that knowledge is a justified belief. By definition, to have knowledge is to be in possession of information that is true because if we "know" something that is not true, we don't really know it but only believe it.

But what is "true"? Perhaps something true corresponds to some form of reality – whether empirical reality or a realm of ideal forms. This is the "correspondence" theory of truth. The nature of truth is a question in metaphysics, but one that clearly lies at the heart of epistemology. Thomas Aquinas gave a succinct statement of correspondence:

"Truth is the conformity of the intellect to the things."

Aquinas also said that real things participate in God's creation, and God is truth. The human intellect, he believed, is able to apprehend the essence of things because of its spiritual, God-participating aspect.

There is, though, a problem with the correspondence definition of truth, as pointed out by Kant. We have to rely on our judgement to tell us whether we have accurately judged the truth of something (whether it corresponds to reality), so we are judging our own judgement. It's not a robust test.

Redefining truth

Søren Kierkegaard divided truths into "objective" and "subjective". Objective truths are things such as the laws of mathematics and other statements about the external world in relation to itself, and statements about the facts of being. Subjective truths are statements about the internal, personal world, the relationship of the individual to the world – the way of being. These vary between individuals and their truth-value is constantly changing and evolving. Subjective truth is dynamic, while objective truth is static.

Nietzsche wrote in *Beyond Good and Evil* (1886), "The falseness of a judgement is to us not necessarily an objection to a judgement. . . . The question is to what extent it is life-advancing, life-preserving, species-preserving, perhaps even species-breeding."

American philosopher John Dewey (1859–1952) held that "truth" as a measure of how well an

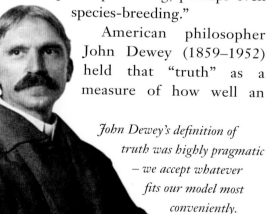

John Dewey's definition of truth was highly pragmatic – we accept whatever fits our model most conveniently.

account or model fits reality is worthless. He suggested instead that we accept as "true" the interpretation of events that proves most useful – that gives us a way of living and working in the world as we find it. He called this state "warranted assertability", avoiding the pretensions and philosophical baggage of the word "truth". But now the genie was out of the bottle – the "truth" didn't have to be "true" any more in the commonsense definition of the word.

The American philosopher Richard Rorty (1931–2007) was influenced by Dewey. He felt that the long philosophical search for foundational values, or *a priori* truths, would never "produce noncontroversial results concerning matters of ultimate concern". He rejected the Cartesian attempt to make philosophy a science, which he felt had led to hundreds of years of debate between rationalists and empiricists, idealists and materialists that had got us nowhere. The idea that the mind is a "theatre of representations", forever dealing with a reality outside itself, was faulty. So too was the later attempt to replace mind in the equation with language, and the earlier model with God in place of science.

In place of intellectually bankrupt traditions, Rorty offered "epistemological behaviourism". The central premise of this is that we know what our society lets us know. What we accept has nothing to do with how well a statement mirrors the world, and everything to do with how well it fits in with what we already believe. Answers as to why we believe what we believe will be found in psychology, sociology or biology, but not philosophy.

Thinkers throughout the ages –

Copernicans, Marxists and modern scientists in one of Rorty's examples – came up with sentences that redescribe reality, such as "the Earth goes round the Sun", "all history is the history of class struggles" and "matter can be changed into energy". These redescriptions were initially seen as false, then accepted as hypotheses, and finally "became accepted, at least within certain communities of inquiry, as obviously true". Since there are no ultimate truths, Rorty felt that truth cannot be a meaningful goal of inquiry. Philosophers should aim instead for the practical matter of "honest justification". Those beliefs that "work", that help in the achievement of a culture's aims, are the ones which can be justified.

What can we say?

For the last 150 years or so, the slipperiness and imprecision of language itself has emerged as a major strand in philosophy. The need to express philosophical thoughts – all thoughts, indeed – in language has led to the concern that what we can say or even think is proscribed by the language we have to use. What we understand of what other people say is distorted by our own understanding of language. In what way does language relate or correspond to any type of reality?

Unfortunately, language is really our only way of communicating with each other. Words have meaning because they have accrued that meaning over time, through use and re-use. With concrete nouns – dog, chair, umbrella, and so on – it's quite easy for us to agree on a meaning, at least at a fairly functional level. Or so it would appear. In fact, there is a lot of extra knowledge we

Just as the "veil of perception" distorts our view of reality, so the inevitable use of language to communicate ideas distorts them in transmission and reception.

need in order to agree: what makes a fox not a dog? How is a parasol not an umbrella? It becomes harder with abstracts and with adjectives, prepositions and other non-concrete words. Words have connotations and implications that are often dependent on the social or intellectual context in which they are used. For example, if I said to my teenage daughter "Granddad is sick", she would know I meant he was unwell. If I said "That jumper is sick", she would know I meant it was a pleasing jumper. But if I said "That video is sick", she would not know whether I meant it was a really good video, or a distasteful video with degrading or offensive content.

A philosopher such as Heidegger – who distrusted and discarded much of the established vocabulary of philosophical discourse – might coin new terms to avoid inappropriate or inconvenient accretions of meaning, but the problem is that no one else would know what those new terms meant. So the philosopher must define new terms, or write in such a way that their meaning becomes apparent – emerges – from the context. There are some coinages in this book – "dough-not", "giraffe-ness", "what/ever" – which illustrate this point.

The "linguistic turn"

The interest in linguistic philosophy began with the work of German mathematician, logician and philosopher Gottlob Frege

(1848–1925). Frege challenged the definition of a proposition that had been accepted since Aristotle formulated it, and recast language in a mathematical model. If we take the sentence "socrates is wise", the Aristotelian (syllogistic) way of describing it is to say it has a subject, "socrates", and a predicate, "is wise". Frege instead separated the sentence into an argument, "socrates", and a function, "is wise". We can take Socrates out and see what kind of word needs to go in its place:

( ) is wise

This is like a mathematical statement in which the arguments can be replaced in a function:

( ) + ( )

As neither the argument nor the function means anything in isolation and the sentence only has meaning in its entirety, it is then

> "When they (my elders) named some object, and accordingly moved towards something, I saw this and I grasped that the thing was called by the sound they uttered when they meant to point it out. Their intention was shown by their bodily movements, as it were the natural language of all peoples: the expression of the face, the play of the eyes. . . . Thus as I heard words repeatedly used in their proper places in various sentences, I gradually learnt to understand what objects they signified; and . . . I used them to express my own desires."
> St Augustine, *Confessions*, I. 8

THE START OF SEMIOTICS

The Swiss linguist Ferdinand de Saussure (1857–1913) is often considered the founder of semiotics, laying important foundations for 20th-century linguistics. He saw language as a system of signs; each word is a sign that can be seen as a signifier-and-signified pairing. The signifier is the spoken (or written) word, a pattern of sounds. The signified is the thing or concept that the word denotes. The pattern of sounds that relates to any particular concept is fundamentally arbitrary. So although we can trace the sound of a word such as "cat" through different languages there is no reason why that sound rather than any other should be linked with the concept of "cat".

Language, though, is greater than the sum of the words that comprise it. It has a structure that can be analysed independently of the words that make it up, and it forms a system by which humans can constitute and articulate their world.

Language is essentially social; it is a shared sign system that, in order to make meaning, needs other people to be able to decode the signs. The sound and meaning (signifier and signified) are both "deposited in the mind" by a speech event. The signifier and signified are like "the front and back of a single sheet of paper". Words are given meaning by virtue of the differences between them and other words – so "male" and "female" require each other in order to be meaningful.

---

clear that context is what bestows meaning. Frege goes further to show that there is a gap between the referent (what is being discussed) and the sense of a sentence. For example, suppose there is a film star called Fifi Ambergris and we are talking about her. I call her "that plastic bimbo" but you call her "that Oscar-winning beauty"; we mean different things (the sense is different) but are referring to the same person (the reference is the same, Fifi Ambergris).

The coiffure of the King of France

The British philosopher Bertrand Russell (1872–1970) was concerned with problems of meaning and reference. He tackled the problem of whether a sentence such as "The present King of France is bald" can be said to be true, false or meaningless. This sentence is said to "not refer" as the subject (the King of France) does not exist.

If we say it is false, that implies the contrary (that the King of France is not bald) is true. But the statement is clearly not true, either. And it is not meaningless in that we can understand what it says.

Russell proposed that such sentences consist of separate claims, which must be separately assessed. In this case, the first proposition (that there is a King of France) is false. Only one claim needs to be false for the whole to be rejected as false, so we can now reject this statement as false. This is the theory of "definite descriptions". It is useful in that it means we can talk meaningfully about things which don't exist.

Wittgenstein v. Augustine

Frege influenced the early work of Ludwig Wittgenstein (1889–1951), one of the most famous philosophers of language. Wittgenstein initially published to great acclaim, then spent his later life renouncing what he had said and trying to come up with a better account.

In his *Tractatus Logico-Philosophicus* (1922), Wittgenstein took issue with what he called the "the Augustinian picture of language". He was not troubled by the magnitude of the figure he was taking on. Although he was only 32 when *Tractatus* was published, Wittgenstein claimed it answered all the questions of philosophy and there was no more to do, then promptly retired from active academic life.

The *Tractatus* tackles the relationship between language, thought and reality. Wittgenstein followed Frege in saying that the meaning of any expression must be determined by the nature of the world – without context, everything is vague and meaningless. And he followed Bertrand Russell in saying that language and the world must be understood in terms of

their constituent parts. But he went further in saying that the underlying structure of sentences must mirror the structure of the world. He said that sentences must be representations – pictures – of possible states of affairs. This is his "picture theory" of language. He denied that the structure of language could be imperfect in terms of its logic. Anything that can be said, he claimed, can be said clearly. Anything that can't be said clearly must be "passed over in silence".

Although initially immensely pleased with *Tractatus*, Wittgenstein later had second thoughts. After going into voluntary exile for a while, he returned to Cambridge in 1929 and set about trying to revise it. For the next twenty years – until he died – he tried to clarify what he had meant and remove confusion, strongly criticizing his earlier work while all around were still praising it.

In *Philosophical Investigations* (1952), published after his death, Wittgenstein reversed his thinking, saying that meaning is not actually dependent on reality, nor is language concerned with representing the world. Words help to elucidate meaning. So, by indicating a dog it helps us to see what the concept "dog" means. By indicating lots of different dogs, it makes the meaning a bit clearer as we can see which features of the dogs are essential to their dog-ness (being brown is not; having four legs generally is, and so on).

He saw that language has many functions and words can be used as tools in different ways – not just to describe things but to ask questions, give orders, insult people and even to lie. The meaning of a word depends on how it is being used at the time – indeed, words are defined by how they are used. His

Astonishingly, Ludwig Wittgenstein (second from left, front row) was in the same elementary school class as Adolf Hitler (right, back row).

notion of a "language-game" rests on this: that meaning is not tied to reality, but must be deduced or untangled from the context in which a word is used. The behavior of language-users both explains and defines the meanings of words.

Speech acts

The British philosopher of language John Austin (1911–60), like Wittgenstein in *Philosophical Investigations*, was interested in how language is used for different purposes – for different kinds of "speech-act", as he called them. In *How to Do Things With Words* (1962), he described three types of speech act. In the first type, words have their literal meaning, saying something about the world. For instance, "the cat sat on the mat" tells us there was a cat and a mat and shows the relationship between them (which one was on top). This he called a "locutionary act". Sometimes, words can serve another function, such as asking a question, making a promise or giving an order – "put the cat on the mat," for instance. This he calls an "illocutionary act". Finally, some utterances are an action. Saying "I

do" at a wedding gets you married; agreeing a deal on a house makes you a house-owner. These are "perlocutionary acts". A speech-act can serve more than one of these functions at a time. "The cat is on the mat!" can mean "get that cat off the precious mat immediately" and then it is an instruction, an illocutionary act. If someone removes the cat as a result, it has worked as a perlocutionary act. Understanding these acts, according to Austin, changes our idea of meaning in language. The first two – locutionary and illocutionary acts – depend on convention and context for us to understand what is meant. If we don't share certain rules of language use with the speaker, we will not necessarily know what is meant.

> *"The only absolute truth is that there are no absolute truths."*
>
> Paul Feyerabend (1924–94)

125

CHAPTER 5

How should we **LIVE?**

"It has been shown that to injure anyone is never just anywhere."

Socrates,
in Plato's *Republic*

"All rational creatures go out upon the sea of life with their minds made up on the common questions of right and wrong."

John Stuart Mill,
Utilitarianism (1861)

"That actions are at once obligatory and at the same time unenforceable is what puts them in the category of the ethical."

David Couzens Hoy
(2004)

Religion often provides a ready-made moral code, enforced by rewards (heaven) and punishment (hell).

Oedipus punishes himself – but is he culpable? He could not avoid killing his father and marrying his mother.

How to live a virtuous life is a question first addressed by Socrates in the 5th century BC and makes up the branch of philosophy known as ethics. Insofar as it is answered with a scheme of acceptable behavior, it is a question in applied ethics. But behind this there are larger questions of how we decide which actions are moral or ethical, whether morality is universal or relative, and how free we are to act in an ethical way. Responsibility for moral action is only meaningful if people can choose how to behave – having both free will in general and the power to be self-determining in their particular circumstances.

Free will and predestination

The question of whether humans are free to make choices or whether we are treading a path already laid out for us and from which we cannot deviate has been asked for thousands of years. While it used to be the gods or fate that were thought to set out our destiny, it is now physics.

The Ancient Greeks and Romans spent a large amount of time, effort and

---

PHILOSOPHERSPEAK: DETERMINISM

Determinism is the belief that everything that will happen in the future is already mapped out (determined) and can't be altered by human actions.

PREDESTINATION PARADOX

Literature often makes use of the "predestination paradox". The story of Oedipus is an example. The king of Thebes, Laius, hears a prophesy that his son will kill him and marry his widow. Hoping to avoid this nasty end, Laius has his baby son, Oedipus, exposed on a mountain with his feet pierced, expecting him to die.

But the baby is rescued and brought up by a shepherd. When he grows up, Oedipus hears the same prophesy and leaves home to avoid killing the shepherd he believes to be his father. Fate is not so easily thwarted, though. On the road, Oedipus meets Laius" entourage. There is a fight (of course – this is Ancient Greece) and Oedipus kills his father. He carries on to Thebes and marries the royal widow, becoming king of Thebes. When he learns that he has, indeed, killed his father and married his mother, he tears out his own eyes.

Science fiction stories and films often use the predestination paradox in the form of a time loop. A character travels backwards in time to prevent a specific event and ends up causing that very event, so the trip through time itself becomes a necessary part of its own history.

Aristotle outlined the problem by describing a sea battle. There might or might not be a sea battle tomorrow, he said. When tomorrow comes, if there is a sea battle, we should be able to say that the previous day it would have been true to say there was going to be a sea battle. So then the battle looks as though it must inevitably happen, and that the future is entirely determined by past truths. But although Aristotle believed most things could be traced to causes, there was still room for some accidents – for "fresh starts" – in the sequence of events. Some of those depend on us, on things we do, and so it appears that we do have some control over events.

The Stoics took a more rigorous line. They believed that what will happen is predetermined (and is for the best). But they clearly allowed sufficient freedom of action that they considered it worth telling people that they should order their thoughts so as to accept this state of affairs. If everything were 100 percent predetermined, a person who was not destined to accept the Stoic position could never accommodate themselves to it.

money on trips to the oracles to find out what was going to happen to them and what they should do about it. Stories such as that of Oedipus – who couldn't avoid killing his father and marrying his mother – underline the perceived impotence of humans in controlling their destiny.

Stoics, such as Chrysippus of Soli, did not think that our actions could have an impact on what happens as everything is predetermined.

This last point highlights the biggest problem with a doctrine of strict determinism: if humans can't affect the course of fate there is no point in acting at all. What will be, will be, regardless of what we do. There is, then, no incentive to do anything difficult. It is a doctrine that can be taken as a wastrel's charter, a licence for indigence and sloth.

Barriers to free action

There are more ways of denying someone free will than saying that everything is predetermined. There are physical constraints: a person can't operate freely if chained up or imprisoned. Some events necessarily follow others for physical reasons – so if you knock over a cup, the water in it will spill out (physical determinism, or causation). For humans, there is psychological compulsion or bullying – trying to constrain the action of another by threats or coercion. And indoctrination or established beliefs can also prevent an individual exploring alternatives or ever considering another path.

God knows what's going on

Belief in an omniscient God has seemed to some to preclude free will. After all, if God knows what is going to happen, including whatever it is you are going to do tomorrow, how can you be free to act as you wish? But God has a nifty trick: he is extra-temporal, existing outside the stream of time. His seeing things does not make them happen, any more than you seeing the Sun rise makes that happen. He observes what happens in an eternal present. This is near enough the argument put forward by the English friar William of Ockham (1288–1348): necessity and possibility are defined relative to a point in time and a set of circumstances, so an event that looks only possible to us may appear as necessary to God.

Shakespeare's Hamlet is a character paralysed by free will; unable to work out the best course of action, he does nothing until events overtake him.

> *"Let some suppose, from what has been said by us, that we say that whatever occurs happens by a fatal necessity, because it is foretold as known beforehand, this too we explain. We have learned from the prophets, and we hold it to be true, that punishments, chastisements, and good rewards, are rendered according to the merit of each man's actions. Now, if this is not so, but all things happen by fate, then neither is anything at all in our own power. For if it is predetermined that this man will be good, and this other man will be evil, neither is the first one meritorious nor the latter man to be blamed. And again, unless the human race has the power of avoiding evil and choosing good by free choice, they are not accountable for their actions."*
>
> Justin Martyr, or St Justin (AD100–c.165)

Damned if you do, and damned if you don't

It might seem that it doesn't much matter whether or not God knows what will happen until we consider the thorny issue of salvation. Many of the Church Fathers – the very early Christian teachers and thinkers – argued that God had given humankind free will. Along with free will comes the responsibility to choose good actions over bad actions, and culpability for the wrong choice. Without freedom, we could not be held responsible for what we did and so could not fairly be punished for sinful behavior.

This seems a fair deal, but the doctrine of original sin derailed it. If we are born sinful, the dice are weighted against us. The so-called Pelagian heresy (after the 4th-century Celtic monk and ascetic Pelagius) addressed the problem. This holds that humankind is not tainted by original sin, that Adam was only setting a bad example and not polluting all who followed him, and that each individual is fully responsible for every one of their sins and for following the teachings of the gospel. Sinners are criminals who have freely chosen depravity when they could have chosen to be virtuous. The virtuous are rewarded for their choice with salvation.

St Augustine, following the Epistle of St Paul, overturned the Pelagian heresy. He argued that all humans are born into

John Calvin was an important figure in Reformation theology, and one of the original proponents of the system later labelled Calvinism.

131

sin, and redemption is only possible through the grace of God. Adam has already condemned all mankind to damnation. Repentance and virtuous living are the only possible paths to salvation, but even then salvation is not guaranteed – we still need divine intervention to save us. The same view was supported by Anselm of Canterbury (1033–1109), Thomas Aquinas, the Scottish cleric John Duns Scotus (1266–1308) and the Protestant reformer Martin Luther.

The French theologian John Calvin was strongly influenced by St Augustine,

If God knows whether you are damned or saved, why bother living an abstemious, virtuous life?

NEUROLOGY AND FREE WILL

A neurological experiment at the Max Planck Institute in Germany in 2008 showed that test subjects" brain signals indicated which hand they were going to use in an experiment seven seconds before the subjects were conscious of having made the decision. It meant that researchers could predict the decision the subjects were going to make and this seemed to bring into question the issue of whether humans truly have freedom of choice in their decision-making. It seems that the feeling of having made a decision could be a physical consequence of something that was not actually an act of free will.

and his doctrine of election is rooted in the belief that God has already chosen those who will be saved by grace. This means that no matter how well or badly we behave, our destiny as elect or not cannot be changed. This seems to suggest that there is no incentive to act well, but those who accepted the doctrine believed acting well revealed that they were among the elect. Keen to find such a sign in themselves, they would eschew sin and depravity. The obvious counter-argument, made by the Dutch humanist Justus Velsius (*c*.1510–*c*.1581), is that if God has allowed some people to be born in the full knowledge that they are headed for eternal damnation and have no way of redeeming themselves then God is a tyrant.

A more liberal view has God giving humans the ability to choose whether to act well or sinfully and then using his veto to save the good ones and letting the bad ones go to hell as they should. Because we are all, technically, damned because of original sin, he is being merciful in saving the good people rather than being mean in damning the bad. But of course, he wrote the rules, and damning unborn people because of someone else's sin long ago seems unreasonable.

God's not looking

Spinoza saw everything as part of the One. As everything that happens is a necessary expression of the nature of the One, free will is effectively removed from humans. He maintained, though, that we experience life as though we were free:

." . . experience tells us clearly that men believe themselves to be free simply because they are conscious of their actions and unconscious of the causes whereby these actions are determined; further, it is plain

Democritus was known as the laughing philosopher because he was said to laugh at human folly.

PHILOSOPHERSPEAK: NORMATIVE ETHICS

Normative ethics deals with which actions are morally right and wrong. There are three main thrusts in the philosophy of normative ethics:

► Virtue ethics focuses on the individual's moral intentions in acting

► Deontology focuses on the rules regarding actions

► Consequentialism focuses on the consequences of an action.

Chaos theory states that any tiny change in a closed system produces wide-ranging consequences. Despite the name, the chain of changes is not chaotic, but just very difficult to predict.

that the dictates of the mind are simply another name for the appetites that vary according to the varying state of the body."

He offered a tiny crumb of freedom, though not of an especially useful sort. Each of us is ruled by our own emotions and appetites and hemmed in by limited understanding. Although we can't escape causal necessity, he suggested that if by reflection we can come to understand our place in the great causal chain we can at least be freed from ignorance.

Physical determinism

The Ancient Greek philosopher Democritus believed that everything happened by necessity and was dictated by the predictable movement of atoms in the void. But he allowed that some atoms swerve in a way that is unpredictable, so creating human souls and an element of freedom.

In some ways, Democritus foreshadowed modern physics. He considered that all matter is made up of atoms ("uncuttables") and that the properties of matter and behavior of atoms mean that the progress of everything is predictable. Modern physics holds that everything can be predicted by physical laws (though we can't precisely predict the future, as our understanding of

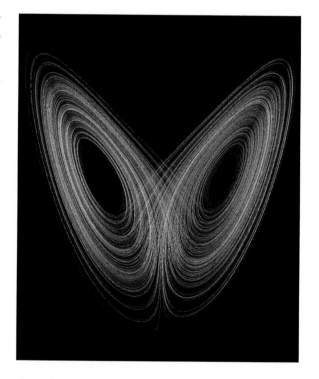

the physical laws is imperfect). This means that we don't have free will unless we believe there is some non-physical animating spirit not subject to those laws. Anyone who subscribes to the view that consciousness is an emergent property of matter is left with the conclusion that we don't have free will – though we have the illusion of it. Without the illusion of free will, we would be frozen into inertia or driven to despair and existential angst.

THE STORY OF SIR GOWTHER

The medieval verse romance *Sir Gowther* tells of a young man who is the child of a demon-rapist and a mortal woman. As an infant and young child, Gowther's inherent evil is manifest. He bites his wet nurses, pushes nuns over cliffs, and indulges in other types of evil behavior. When he is a little older, someone tells him that his perversity is the result of his parentage – that he is only evil because he is half-demon. Gowther is frustrated by this explanation and determines to be truly perverse by rebelling against his nature. He turns to doing good acts.

The question is, are his acts of charity and benevolence of any moral value, given that he does them out of a desire to be perverse and unnatural? For a virtue ethicist such as Kant, they are *not* moral. For a deontological ethicist, they *are* moral as Gowther is following the rules – not biting people, not pushing nuns off cliffs and so on. And for a consequentialist, too, they *are* moral because good results from them; Gowther carries out good deeds from which people benefit.

How do we make a good life?

A few people (we call them psychopaths) live in such a way as to bring benefit only to themselves, regardless of the welfare of or cost to others. So how should we live? Even the term "benefit" is up for grabs. For some, maximizing pleasure and minimizing pain defines benefit. For others, the greatest benefit is salvation, which often involves renouncing physical pleasure. And for still others it is intellectual fulfilment or feeling at one with a universal spirit.

If we do not accept free will, how are we to treat criminals? If they cannot be held responsible for their behaviour, can they be punished?

Socrates and the start of ethics

The pre-Socratic philosophers were more concerned with "meta-ethical" issues such as the nature of virtue than with the question of how to live virtuously. Socrates was the

THE PROBLEM OF IGNORANCE

Socrates" method ignores one important point: often people know what is good for them and still don't do it, or still do what is bad for them. There is a tendency to seek short-term secure benefit (the pleasure of another glass of wine or an extra cake, or the excitement of an extra-marital affair, for example) over long-term possible harm (hangovers, obesity, heart and liver disease, divorce). Socrates would say that wine-swilling, cake-scoffing adulterers are ignorant – they have not fully understood the implications of their actions. Weakness and risk-taking influence our behavior. In fact, the problem of why people continue to do something they know is wrong greatly troubled Aristotle and Plato and neither had a satisfactory answer.

In his *Confessions* (CE398), St Augustine described stealing pears as a boy. He did not need the pears, and indeed had nicer pears at home. He admitted that he stole them precisely because he knew that he should not – because he was attracted by sin. He recognized that often the sinner "hates the thing itself because he knows that it is evil; and yet he does it because he is bent on doing it".

St Augustine accounted for this by saying that it is the taint of original sin that we must battle against.

Socrates would put self-indulgent harmful behaviour down to ignorance.

first to take a more practical interest in how we ought to live, and what a "good life" might be – the concerns of *normative ethics*. He has been called the first philosopher of ethics, and his thinking had a long-lasting and wide-ranging influence on Western ethical philosophy. Indeed, the doctrine of "virtue ethics" began with Socrates.

Socrates believed that well-informed people will naturally act well – if they know what is good and what is evil, they will choose the good course of action. He argued that knowledge, and self-knowledge in particular, is the root of morality and that all crime and evil-doing are the result of ignorance. As virtue leads to happiness, the wise person will be moral and therefore happy.

We all seek what is best for us and is in our own interest.

▶ If we know what is good for us, we will act accordingly and benefit.

▶ If we act in a way that brings us harm, we are mistaken in our idea of what is good, because no one willingly seeks their own harm.

▶ Virtue can be equated with knowledge and ignorance with evil.

Socrates" debating of ethical questions often led him into conflict with the elders of Athens, who accused him of corrupting the minds of the wealthy youth with revolutionary and unorthodox ideas. Although he left no written works, his ideas are recorded by his pupil Plato and demonstrated in the way he lived his life.

Striving towards happiness

Aristotle followed Socrates in promoting a practical type of philosophy. His *Nichomachean Ethics* is one of the most important works on ethics in the history of Western philosophy. Aristotle looked at how people should live, and how society should be organized through laws and political structures so as to enable virtuous living. He identified five ways people seek happiness:

▶ The slavish pursuit of pleasure – this is how most people think of happiness.

▶ Money-making – this is generally an intermediate aim, sought by people who are in pursuit of something else.

▶ Having virtue but being inactive, even suffering misfortunes with patience.

▶ Through politics.

▶ Through contemplation.

Aristotle believed the first two ways are very inferior types of happiness and saw little point in inactive virtue. True happiness, he decided, is achieved by being a "serious" person – one who has thought clearly and acts honorably, who is engaged actively with friends, family and his community and who pursues virtue. It is the internal quality of virtue that defines someone as morally good.

For Aristotle, living a virtuous life went hand-in-hand with self-realization – with fulfilling one's potential, examining life and living thoughtfully. This accords with his general teleological approach: that everything is striving to fulfil its purpose. He saw virtue in moderation. So the virtue of courage, for instance, is the moderate path between recklessness and cowardice. Wisdom was very close to virtue in Aristotle's schema.

The dog in a jar

If Socrates caused trouble for himself then another Greek philosopher, Diogenes (400–325 BCE), went even further. According to

Plato, Diogenes out-Socratesed Socrates – "a Socrates gone mad", Plato called him. A contemporary of Aristotle, it seems that Diogenes was both charismatic and enigmatic. No works by him survive, and it seems unlikely that he recorded his ideas in writing.

Diogenes distanced himself from the intellectual pretensions of other philosophers, adopting a straightforward and extremely ascetic approach to virtue. He believed that happiness was attained by living "according to nature" – satisfying the body's most basic needs in the simplest ways. His methods of promoting his ideas were the opposite of the intellectual provocation of Socrates. Among other controversial stunts, Diogenes is said to have claimed that to be fulfilled, one must give up all property, all possessions, all family ties and social values, as all emotional and psychological attachments are distractions and illusions. Called "the dog" in recognition of his vagrant lifestyle, Diogenes practiced what he preached, making a living by begging, and wearing only the simplest of clothes.

But just giving up material and personal attachments was not enough. Loyal followers of Diogenes were expected to attack society to help free others from its shackles, and should deliberately put themselves in the way of ridicule and abuse to stay well-practiced in emotional detachment. Mastery of the self, or "self-sufficiency" would, according to Diogenes, lead to happiness and freedom.

What if everyone did that?

Critics have complained that Diogenes" lifestyle is self-indulgent, a criticism that can be levelled at all ascetics who depend on the generosity of others for their existence. Clearly, as a philosophical position it can't be extended far. If too many people followed Diogenes" example, there would be too few productive people to support the burden of ascetic nomads and jar-dwellers and society would collapse. That would make it impossible for anyone, including Diogenes, to concentrate on mastery of the self. Diogenes" philosophy is essentially elitist – it can't be followed by everyone, or even by many.

Diogenes attracted a loose collection of followers called the Cynics, and around CE1 Cynicism resurfaced in Rome. The name did not have the overtones that the word "cynic" has now, but meant something closer to asceticism. There were good reasons for the popularity of Cynicism,

> "The pursuit of pleasure is a life fit only for beasts."
> Aristotle, *Nicomachean Ethics*

DIOGENES OF SINOPE (c.404–325BCE)

Accounts of Diogenes" life are not wholly reliable, but they are entertaining. He was born in the Greek colony of Sinope on the Black Sea coast and worked with his father, Hicesias, a banker. He was exiled after being involved in a scandal to do with defacing coinage, and moved to Athens. Legend reports that he pestered the philosopher Antisthenes, a pupil of Socrates, to be his tutor, but there is no real evidence that the two ever met. Diogenes lived in a stone jar in the market place, making money by begging, and gave up as many possessions as he could. One anecdote says that after seeing a child scoop up water with his hands he broke his own drinking bowl in half as he realized that the bowl was a luxury he could do without.

When Plato quoted Socrates" definition of a man as a "featherless biped", Dioegenes is said to have responded by taking a plucked chicken to the Academy and presenting it as a man. Plato then revised the definition of a man to include "broad, flat nails".

According to legend, when Diogenes was in Corinth, he witnessed the triumphal return of Alexander the Great. Intrigued by the fact that Diogenes took not the slightest notice of him, Alexander went to see the philosopher and found him lying in the sun. When Alexander asked if he wanted anything, Diogenes replied: "Yes – stand a little out of my sun."

though. It coincided, in both Greece and Rome, with times of economic difficulty and social unrest. The idea that the one thing of real value is mastery of the self, which can't be taken away by misfortune, was attractive when material goods, social stability and family were all under threat.

Putting up with things

Stoicism marked a similar but less extreme way of relinquishing temporal concerns. Beginning with Zeno of Citium (334–c.262BCE) and continuing until the time of the Roman philosopher Seneca (4BCE–CE65) and the Greek philosopher Epictetus (CE55–135), Stoicism taught a disdain for and disengagement from temporal woes and problems, and that destructive emotions (such as misery, envy and hate) are the result of errors in judgement. The way to happiness, open to the sage, is through moral and intellectual perfection. The object of humankind is to live in accord with nature, which means to live by reason, as we are all part of a universal single, reasoning substance. The Stoics did not seek to deny or avoid emotions, but to channel or transform them to produce a clear-thinking calm through self-discipline and reason.

Seneca had a more pragmatic bent than many. He promoted a simple life devoted to virtue and reason, and insisted that the only good is virtue. He taught that doing the right thing is of paramount importance – nothing else really matters. Seneca believed that we each have an internal god guiding us along the path set out for us by providence and that the only way to attain happiness is to follow this inner guide, acting in accord with our true nature, and being content with our lot. Altruism and simple living were essential to Seneca's idea of morality.

The Roman philosopher Boethius (CE480–*c*.525) was consoled by reading Seneca's writings while in prison. His own *Consolation of Philosophy* agrees with Seneca and the Stoics in promoting a disengagement or aloofness from the vicissitudes of fortune and a focus on reason and virtue. Boethius, a Christian, wrote a Platonic and Stoic text that accorded with Christianity but did not mention the Christian God. The *Consolation* was something of a bridge between Seneca and Thomas Aquinas, Boethius being both the last Roman philosopher and the first scholastic.

All for pleasure

Plato, Seneca and Aristotle were among the Classical authorities who were accommodated by medieval Christian philosophy.

If Diogenes was extreme in the degree to which he spurned worldly pleasures, Epicurus went a long way in the other direction. He was not really interested in abstruse metaphysical speculation, but in a practical philosophy of life. He taught the pursuit of happiness, which he considered to be achieved by avoiding both physical and mental pain. Of the two types, he considered mental pain to be worse. Physical pain is temporary and can be brought under control, or it results in death, at which point it no longer matters. (He did not believe in a soul that persisted after death.) The mental pain of fear or anxiety, though, could continue unabated, festering into psychological illness.

Even though Epicurus taught the

Boethius" Consolation of Philosophy, written while he was in prison in 524, is the philosophical bridge between the ancient world and the Middle Ages. Here Philosophy instructs Boethius on the role of God.

pursuit of pleasure, he was not a hedonist. He realized that over-indulgence could lead to painful consequences and so encouraged temperance. He suffered poor health himself, and was not wealthy; to accuse him of promoting decadence and promiscuity, as the Stoic philosopher Epictetus did, would be unfair. Epicurus taught that wisdom was the greatest virtue as it enables a person to distinguish between pleasures which should be sought and those which should be avoided. He believed that no one could be truly happy unless they were virtuous, as virtue leads to pleasurable consequences and to the absence of pain and fear.

Ethics and Christianity

Although Boethius" *Consolation of Philosophy* is not an explicitly Christian work, it was immensely popular and influential throughout the Middle Ages. An accomplished scholar fully acquainted with Plato, Aristotle and his other predecessors, Boethius covers a lot of ground in the *Consolation*, including the issues of free will and predestination, the existence of evil and

TOO MUCH, TOO YOUNG

For true hedonism, we need to look to Aristippus of Cyrene (c.435–c.356BCE), a wayward pupil of Socrates. The Cyrenaics believed in indulging in every available pleasure while the opportunity presented itself. They showed no concern for the future and believed pleasure to be the only good.

how to live a virtuous life. The book takes the form of a debate between Boethius in his prison cell and Lady Philosophy, who answers his tricky questions.

Throughout the Middle Ages, Christian philosophers had less room to manoeuvre than their classical predecessors because the Bible is prescriptive about virtue and how people should live. St Thomas Aquinas accommodated Aristotelian ethics into the Christian schema. He accepted Aristotle's teleological view that an act is judged to be good or bad according to whether or not it furthers the subject's aim of fulfilment. At the same time, he had to accept that ultimate fulfilment, for a Christian, is salvation and that can't be achieved by the individual alone – it needs God's grace to perfect our nature.

Being is being good

Working from Augustine and Aristotle, Aquinas said that everything that exists must partake of some goodness:

► There are two types of substance: corruptible and incorruptible. Incorruptible substances are superior to corruptible substances.

► An incorruptible substance, by definition, cannot have any of its goodness removed, so we don't need to think about it.

► A corruptible substance can have some goodness removed, as that's how it is corrupted.

► If a corruptible substance didn't have any goodness, it couldn't have any removed. Therefore all corruptible substances have some goodness in them.

Aristippus of Cyrene would have been happy in today's culture of partying.

- If a substance had no goodness, none could be removed, so it would be incorruptible.
- If an incorruptible substance can have no goodness, a thing could become better by losing all its goodness and becoming incorruptible.
- That would mean a thing could improve by becoming worse, which is clearly nonsense. So therefore it must be the case that there are no things that exist and lack goodness, and so there is some good in everything that exists.

But being and goodness are not the same thing. Things can be more or less good (it is a relative term) but they either exist or they don't (it's an absolute). To address this problem, Aquinas came up with a type of being that he called "relative being". A thing "is" more or less insofar as it is closer to the perfect essence of what that thing should be. So, for instance, a hatchling is less of a bird than a fully fledged bird, as it can't do all the things associated with full bird-ness such as flying, laying eggs, making nests, rearing young and so on. A fully grown bird is therefore a "better" bird than a hatchling. Similarly, a person is a better person if they act with morality, dignity, compassion and thought than if they are selfish, immoral and act without considering what they are doing and the impact it will have.

The same for all or different for each?

A code such as Christianity does not leave much space for individuals to come up with their own moral schema. For the thousand years or so following Boethius, Christian philosophers could do little with ethics. But by the 16th century, when the humanist Michel de Montaigne was writing, the Church had lost its monopoly.

Montaigne was the first philosopher to promote cultural relativism, accepting that different behavior and values are lauded in different cultures. There is no reason to suppose that one culture's way of doing things is better than another's, or even that humans are innately superior to other animals. This was quite revolutionary thinking at the time; the general belief that European Christian culture was the "right" way was the excuse for slaughtering, subjugating and indoctrinating the indigenous populations of North and South America, who were considered "savages". Of course, those who criticized the "barbarous" practices of the "savages" were often content to endorse or turn a blind eye to judicial torture in Europe (*plus ça change*, we might think).

Even so, Montaigne didn't believe that all customs were equally acceptable, and nor were all individuals equally in thrall to their own cultural norms. He urged every individual to examine what is expected in their social context and make a decision, based on universal and inherent standards bestowed by God, about whether to accept the prevailing values. No universal code is necessary, as we can each look at different ways of doing things and make our own

> *"The laws of conscience, which we say are born of nature, are born of custom. Each man, holding in inward veneration the opinions and behaviour approved and accepted around him"*
> Michel de Montaigne, *On Custom*

Cuauhtémoc, the last ruler of the Aztecs, was defeated by the Spanish in 1521 and tortured in an attempt to get him to reveal the whereabouts of the gold the Spaniards believed he had. Spanish atrocities in South America went far beyond the routine cruelty of war in Europe.

judgement about what is appropriate and best in any context. We should all, he felt, remain in constant dialogue and reflection to make the right choices.

Montaigne accepted that there were a few universal standards, such as "reason" and "nature", that were defined by God. These can help us to exercise our judgement. Montaigne's philosophy had an impact on Pascal and Descartes. Descartes in particular was heavily influenced by Montaigne's emphasis on self-education and the garnering of experience to inform philosophical reflection.

This approach, devolving responsibility to the individual, is the hallmark of humanism. It does not preach either indulgence or asceticism as a route to self-discovery and virtue, but emphasizes the individual's own power and responsibility to find a path to a better life.

PHILOSOPHERSPEAK: CULTURAL RELATIVISM

Cultural relativism is the belief that values and moral or legal codes are variable according to cultural context. What is acceptable in one culture is not in another, and consequences follow from this. In Muslim countries, for instance, some forms of Western dress are considered immodest.

Montaigne's belief that humans are not innately superior to all other species is shared by animal rights activists.

Kant took almost the opposite view, presenting morality as an objective scheme that must be arrived at by "pure practical reason". Instead of each person assessing circumstances and custom and referring to their own moral compass, he believed that right and wrong are absolute and cannot be decided empirically, by referring to experience.

In *Critique of Practical Reason*, Kant explained what he called "the categorical imperative". This is a type of universal moral law that he formulated several times. In essence, it takes the question

that undid Diogenes" plan for a moral life and uses it as a standard by which we can measure any behavior – "what if everyone did that?" In Kant's words, "act by that maxim which you can at the same time will as a universal law". If each act were extended to a universal moral law (that is, something which everyone complied with), would it work? If everyone avoided paying taxes, the country would be bankrupt, so avoiding paying taxes is not acceptable behavior. This removes the question from a purely moral dilemma and makes it more rational. It provides a moral compass that even someone totally lacking in empathy could use. But then, is it a moral choice if not made for moral reasons? When does a moral act stop being moral and just become pragmatism?

Kant did take account of this. For him, an act could be moral only if it was performed out of a sense of moral duty, or respect for the moral law: "The concept of a worth which thwarts my self-love." In Kant's second formulation of the categorical imperative, he said that we must always treat humanity as an end as well as a means. This

"Act only according to that maxim whereby you can, at the same time, will that it should become a universal law."
"Act in such a way that you treat humanity, whether in your own person or in the person of any other, never merely as a means to an end, but always at the same time as an end."

Immanuel Kant, *Groundwork of the Metaphysic of Morals* (1785)

145

means that a person (including oneself) can't be simply used – so no one can own a slave just to get work done, or send troops to be slaughtered at one location to distract an enemy from another location.

For Kant, it is not the consequences of an act that make it moral, but the intention behind the act. We can't deduce good will from the outcome of an act. A person could act with bad intentions and their act could have beneficial consequences. Similarly, a person might act benevolently, but what they do might have unforeseen bad consequences.

The highest "good", according to Kant, must be "good in itself" (intrinsic good) and "good without qualification" – it must never make a situation morally worse. The only good he found that fitted the criteria was "good will": an act must be carried out with good will in order to be genuinely moral, and that means acting out of respect for the moral law. Insofar as Kant's morality demands that people follow rules, it is deontological. There is an element of virtue ethics, though, in that virtuous intention must also be present.

Versions of Kant's theory of moral duty have been widely upheld and defended by philosophers right up to the present day. In its uncompromising insistence on never using a person "merely as a means to an end", Kant's scheme is hard to implement. Some modern philosophers have tried to

In the Victorian children's story The Water Babies, *Mrs Doasyouwouldbedoneby is the embodiment of Kant's categorical imperative.*

temper it to make it more viable. Harvard professor of philosophy Frances Kamm has described the "principle of permissible harm" in which harm to a small number of people may be balanced against benefit to a large number of people under certain circumstances. So while it would be wrong in both Kamm's and Kant's scheme to kill someone to harvest their organs and save four other lives, it would be permissible in Kamm's scheme to kill a gunman to save the people he was about to slaughter.

PHILOSOPHERSPEAK: DEONTOLOGICAL ETHICS
A moral scheme based on duty is deontological (from *deon*, duty).

Utilitarian ethics

There is nothing personal or sentimental about Kant's approach to ethics, but at least he had wrested the issue away from religion. The dissociation of ethics from Christianity allowed a change of focus. Instead of acting morally in order to secure salvation (or to prove one's status as one of the elect), acting morally became part of a wider social responsibility.

The British social reformer Jeremy Bentham (1748–1832) is best known today as a political philosopher, but his political

Kant ruled against cruelty to animals because humans have a duty to nurture a sense of compassion. Brutality towards others, whether human or animals, deadens compassion and so violates that duty.

"Nature has placed mankind under the governance of two sovereign masters, pain and pleasure. . . . They govern us in all we do, in all we say, in all we think: every effort we can make to throw off our subjection will serve but to demonstrate and confirm it. In words a man may pretend to abjure their empire, but in reality he will remain subject to it all the while."

Jeremy Bentham, *An Introduction to the Principles of Morals and Legislation* (1789)

ideas overlap with his ideas about ethics. Born in Houndsditch, London, Bentham was a child prodigy who started to learn Latin at the age of three and went to Queen's College, Oxford at the age of twelve. He trained as a lawyer and was called to the bar, but never practiced – the over-complex language and conflicting

> *"It is the greatest happiness of the greatest number that is the measure of right and wrong."*
>
> Jeremy Bentham,
> *A Fragment on Government* (1776)

principles of the law put him off. Instead, he undertook a philosophical investigation into the basis of law, morals and politics. Like Epicurus, Bentham believed that people are driven towards that which they desire (pleasure, or happiness) and shun that which they fear (pain). By applying this principle to society, he developed and popularized a system known as "utilitarianism". He hoped to draw up a complete code of law based on utilitarian principles, which he called a "Pannomion".

The simple moral rule that emerges from Bentham's findings is that we should do whatever will maximize pleasure and minimize pain. Bentham's plan, though, is quantitative in nature: whatever brings the most pleasure in total is the best course of action, even though that may involve bringing pain to a few people. Bentham did not

shirk from quantifying pain and pleasure, even developing a "felicific calculus", an algorithm for calculating the net pain and pleasure generated by an action or rule.

Although the first to formulate utilitarianism into a full ethical and political scheme, Bentham was not the first to express the idea that the morality of an action can be measured by how much pleasure or pain it brings to people. The philosopher Francis Hutcheson wrote in *An Inquiry into the Original of Our Ideas of Beauty and Virtue* (1725) "that action is best, which procures the greatest happiness for the greatest

Jeremy Bentham was a child prodigy who later developed the principle of utilitarianism.

"The day may come when the rest of the animal creation may acquire those rights which never could have been witholden from them but by the hand of tyranny. The French have already discovered that the blackness of the skin is no reason a human being should be abandoned without redress to the caprice of a tormentor. It may one day come to be recognized that the number of the legs, the villosity [hairiness] of the skin, or the termination of the os sacrum [end of the spine] are reasons equally insufficient for abandoning a sensitive being to the same fate. . . . The question is not, Can they reason? nor, Can they talk? but, Can they suffer?"

Jeremy Bentham, *Introduction to the Principles of Morals and Legislation* (1789)

numbers; and that, worst, which, in like manner, occasions misery". He, too, offered algorithms "to compute the Morality of any Actions". His contemporary John Gay took the idea a step further in 1731, claiming that it is the will of God that people should be happy and so we are obliged by religion to pursue the path that will lead to the greatest pleasure for the greatest number.

Taken to extremes, utilitarianism could allow the life of one person to be sacrificed to bring pleasure to many, though this is something Bentham ruled against by allowing that the legal system would protect individuals against such an abuse. The law, he said, "provides the basic framework of social interaction by delimiting spheres of personal inviolability within which individuals can form and pursue their own conceptions of well-being". It is a problem

The pleasure of the large number of spectators outweighs the suffering of the dying victim, making the Roman games theoretically acceptable in a rigidly utilitarian scheme. Bentham avoided such conclusions.

DEAD, BUT NOT GONE

As he requested in his will, Bentham's body was dissected as part of a public anatomy lecture and his skeleton formed into an "auto-icon" padded with straw and dressed in his clothes. The shoddy mummification of his head produced a macabre result and a wax effigy of his head, embellished with his own hair, was used instead. The auto-icon usually sits in the South Cloisters of the main building of University College London but has, on occasion, attended meetings of the College Council, recorded as "present but not voting". The mummified head, originally displayed in the same case as the auto-icon, is now locked in a secure location.

that utilitarianism still has not solved.

One of Bentham's students, John Stuart Mill (1806–73), developed utilitarianism further, both in ethics and politics. He divided pleasures into higher and lower categories. Needless to say, the higher pleasures are intellectual, sophisticated and cultural while the lower pleasures are carnal and physical.

Assessing which pleasures fall into each category, and how much people desire one pleasure or another, Mill has to fall back on crowd-sourcing: "The sole evidence it is possible to produce that anything is desirable, is that people do actually desire it." This lays him open to several criticisms, including the "fallacy of equivocation" – saying something is desirable (people desire it) means it is desirable in another sense (it is to be desired). It's just as well he's not around now, or Mill would quickly find himself in the untenable position of considering *X-Factor* to be morally good.

Writing in 1977, the economist John

Harsanyi (1920–2000) managed to side-step this issue by saying that the choices we should take account of are those made when people are in full possession of all the facts and so when they are most likely to be rational, and not subject to extreme emotional states. He also excluded from the crowd-sourcing anyone with antisocial ideas of what is pleasurable (such as sadists).

> "It is better to be a human being dissatisfied than a pig satisfied; better to be Socrates dissatisfied than a fool satisfied. And if the fool, or the pig, are of a different opinion, it is because they only know their own side of the question."
>
> John Stuart Mill, *Utilitarianism* (1861)

How do we choose?

It's all very well crowd-sourcing morality, but it's good to have some idea about how the results have been achieved. The English philosopher and economist Henry Sidgwick (1838–1900) aimed to explore the methods of everyday moral reasoning – how we arrive at decisions about moral behavior, and whether there can be a rational basis on which to make such decisions. His book *The Methods of Ethics* (1874) became one of the classics of moral philosophy.

Sidgwick considered a "method of ethics" to be "any rational procedure by which we determine what individual human beings "ought" to do – or what it is "right"

Small children have a naturally egoistic approach which can make them look selfish, but the capacity to imagine someone else's feelings comes with the development of "theory of mind". Then, altruism becomes possible.

for them to do – or to seek to realize by voluntary action." Of course, people follow different principles when deciding what to do, but he said their "methods" can be grouped according to three basic approaches: *egoism*, *utilitarianism* and *intuitionism*.

Egoism, or egoistic hedonism, deems an action to be more or less moral depending on how happy it makes the person performing it: "The rational agent regards quantity of consequent pleasure and pain to himself as alone important in choosing between alternatives of action; and seeks always the greatest attainable surplus of pleasure over pain."

Utilitarianism, or universalistic hedonism, measures the morality of an action according to its effect on the general happiness of all: "The conduct which . . . is objectively right, is that which will produce the greatest amount of happiness on the whole . . . taking into account all whose happiness is affected by the conduct."

Intuitionism ignores the concept of happiness altogether, and holds that we must simply conform to "certain rules or dictates of Duty". It works on the assumption that we can see instinctively which actions are right in themselves, independent of their consequences: "The moral judgements that men habitually pass on one another in ordinary discourse imply . . . that duty is usually not a difficult

thing for an ordinary man to know, though various seductive impulses may make it difficult for him to do it."

As Sidgwick examined the relationship between intuitionism and the "morality of common sense", the ethical guidelines that guide people's everyday behavior, he found that common-sense morality is to some extent "unconsciously utilitarian". Utilitarianism rests on intuitive moral principles. He concluded that intuitionism and utilitarianism can be integrated into a single ethical system: "such abstract moral principles as we can admit to be really self-evident . . . seem to be required to furnish a rational basis for [a utilitarian] system."

Although he had reconciled the second two methods, egoism remained outside the fold. Egoism also seems to reflect reason

Henry Sidgwick found conflicting ethical impulses, both based in common sense.

and common sense – but it is the opposite of utilitarianism, which might require a person to sacrifice their own happiness, or even their own life, for the greater happiness of society.

Sidgwick acknowledged that few people are as concerned with the pleasure or pain of humankind generally as with that of themselves and their nearest and dearest. He was left with two conflicting principles, utilitarianism and egoism, which are irreconcilable but both based on common sense and valid reasoning. When utilitarian reason makes harsh demands on us, self-interested reason might rightly lead us to object. Sidgwick admitted that the conflict remains insoluble without involving God and some notion of divine rewards and punishments, which he was unwilling to do. He ended the first edition of his book on a despairing note:

"The Cosmos of Duty is . . . reduced to a Chaos; and the prolonged effort of the human intellect to frame a perfect ideal of rational conduct is seen to have been foredoomed to inevitable failure."

Starting over

Friedrich Nietzsche saw a similar failure in the moral codes that had so far evolved. His answer to the problem was to overturn all existing moral structures and start afresh. He located the fundamental driving force of the individual in the need to dominate and control external forces and take charge of personal destiny, yet for many people life circumstances prevent them from doing this. The moral codes that have evolved have done so as a result of trying to accommodate our inability to take control and be self-determining, or even to avoid acknowledging it. They exist to bind and control the striving will of the individual.

Nietzsche traced the predominant moral schemas of Europe, whether Classical or Christian, to the behavior of masters and slaves, or overlords and the oppressed. Moral good and evil are based on the values admired by those who had the upper hand in society (the masters), which are seen as either desirable (by the masters) or evil (by the slaves). In Homeric Greece

According to Nietzsche, slaves and other exploited workers are drawn to religions in which their suffering is considered a badge of virtue and a passport to salvation.

Nietzsche's philosophy, which saw the demise of Christianity and rise of individual power as good things, was appropriated by the leaders of Nazi Germany.

and other social structures marked by a master-slave dichotomy or hierarchical class structure, the life-affirming attributes such as power, physical strength, health and wealth are considered good by those in power. The opposite characteristics are life-denying: poverty, powerlessness, sickness. These are bad. This Nietzsche terms master-morality, though strictly speaking there is no moral position assigned to the characteristics labelled as good or bad – they are rather desirable and undesirable states or properties.

It is the slaves who turn it into a properly "moral" system. The attributes of the oppressors (which the masters consider good) are deemed evil by the slaves. The characteristics that the underclass is forced to adopt in order to shirk their responsibility to free themselves from oppression are deemed morally good (the characteristics the masters consider bad). So cruelty, worldliness, selfishness, aggression and wealth are seen as evil, and humility, poverty, selflessness, submission and piety are seen as good. By relabelling the marks of their powerlessness as virtues, the slaves are able to endure their lot, but avoid the obligation to remedy it. Instead of seeing poverty and powerlessness as social ills, they label them as morally good and then don't try to be rid of them.

Nietzsche saw the tension between master- and slave-moralities as the cause of rising nihilism in Christian Europe. "God is dead," he said – suggesting that nihilism has triumphed, or will triumph. Religious belief was, he felt, a bulwark against nihilism, and without it we struggle to find meaning or to forge a moral code. Nihilism easily leads to despair. But it is also the first step towards a culture with solid foundations, since that depends on overcoming nihilism:

"I praise, I do not reproach, [nihilism's] arrival. I believe it is one of the greatest crises, a moment of the deepest self-reflection of humanity. Whether man recovers from it, whether he becomes master of this crisis, is a question of his strength!"

Nietzsche hoped that the foundations of the new morality could be built amid the rubble of Christianity and nihilism. But for Nietzsche, there was no absolute moral law.

The value-systems that societies produce vary according to their own circumstances and needs, and none is intrinsically better than any other. He believed that it was the act of developing and adhering to a code of values that was the important point, the defining act of a civilized society, and not the content of that code. This view, called "perspectivism", was adopted by some later philosophers, including Martin Heidegger, who developed it into full cultural relativism.

Meta-ethics

From the middle of the 19th century, the Christian fabric of Europe began to unravel more rapidly. Since the Enlightenment, serious thinkers had begun to question the belief in God that they had been brought up with, and although many kept it after careful examination, more and more rejected it or found that it did not answer their needs. Those who, like Spinoza, came up with a different type of theism had to rethink morality. Those who, like Nietzsche, cast off religion altogether as oppressive and misguided needed a completely new basis for morality.

This chapter has been largely concerned with normative ethics – how people should behave. But the beginning of the 20th century saw philosophy taking a step backwards, away from normative ethics, and trying to gain an overview with "meta-ethics" – an investigation of what we mean when we talk about right and wrong and how we can make moral judgements.

The English philosopher George Edward Moore (1873–1958) comes like a breath of fresh air after the brain-strangling contortions that some earlier philosophers performed. Moore proposed that common sense is no bad thing, and can often be trusted. So, for instance, you or I can more readily accept that we existed yesterday than that we need someone like Descartes to help us prove we existed yesterday. Moore – like many people – thought a lot of philosophy was unnecessary nonsense. Many questions about meaning are not asked in everyday life, though the relationship between concepts and their definitions is important in philosophy. In this, he sparked some of the major themes of 20th-century philosophy, including the preoccupation with language.

In *Principia Ethica* (1903), Moore is concerned with the meta-ethical question of what we mean by "good" rather than which actions might be deemed to be good. He says that "good" can't be broken down, but is "a simple notion, just as "yellow" is a simple notion; that, just as you cannot, by any manner of means, explain to anyone who does not already know it, what yellow is, so you cannot explain what good is."

"Good", he said, is something of which we are intuitively aware. We know it is good to be kind to other people and bad to be cruel to them. We don't really need an explanation of why, and so he rejects both Kant's view that ethical judgements are accessible to reason and the utilitarian view. A judgement of what is "good" is always subjective, a value judgement. On the whole, we agree a lot of the time. We disagree over points of detail, of course. We might all agree that it's wrong to kill people generally. Some people will hold the view, though, that judicial killing is acceptable, or that abortion is acceptable, or that euthanasia is acceptable. These details are the material of "applied ethics". Because good cannot be defined acceptably, Moore concluded that ethics can have no basis in either science or metaphysics.

Ethics in daily life

Applied ethics, the application of ethics to everyday life, is what we are engaged in when asking questions such as "do animals have rights?" or "should we assassinate dictators?" The 20th century saw a proliferation of works on specific areas such as bioethics, animal rights and business ethics.

The usual methods of *normative ethics* (virtue ethics, deontological ethics and utilitarian ethics) approach ethical questions from very different starting points. One of the consequences of the fragmentation in theoretical

Is it ethical to assassinate dictators, such as Saddam Hussein?

moral codes has been that there are many accepted but often conflicting viewpoints in modern society. The work of ethics committees and other bodies concerned with making ethical judgments is harder now than it would have been at a time when a universal moral order imposed by the Bible held sway.

One way of dealing with the plurality of theoretical positions is to adopt a method of case-based reasoning, called *casuistry*. It has its origins in Aristotle, and was briefly popular

in the 16th and 17th centuries. Moore was sympathetic towards casuistry: "Casuistry is the goal of ethical investigation. It cannot be safely attempted at the beginning of our studies, but only at the end." After more than half a century of post-Moorean philosophy, casuistry resurfaced in the 1960s as a usable method in applied ethics, and became more prevalent following the ground-breaking work of the American biomedical ethicist Albert Jonsen (born 1931) and the British philosopher Stephen Toulmin (1922–2009),

The Abuse of Casuistry: A History of Moral Reasoning (1988). This approach tackles each individual case in the context of its own circumstances. It works from the known facts and likely consequences, rather than starting from a theoretical code (though it still has to operate within the law). An example of its application is in deciding whether to withdraw life-support from a very sick patient. Because it is not rule-based, it can result in opposite rulings on cases that look very similar.

Ethical resistance – ethics for the 21st century

Post-structuralist and post-modernist philosophers denied the possibility of an objective or even a subjective moral code, saying that all actions must be seen in their own context and in relation to others. In practice, this produces casuistry, with

Ethical resistance consists of non-violent pressure on bodies that the resisters consider oppressive, exploitative or morally reprehensible in some other way.

> "The ethical resistance of the powerless others to our capacity to exert power over them is therefore what imposes unenforceable obligations on us. The obligations are unenforceable precisely because of the other's lack of power. That actions are at once obligatory and at the same time unenforceable is what put them in the category of the ethical. Obligations that were enforced would, by the virtue of the force behind them, not be freely undertaken and would not be in the realm of the ethical."
>
> David Couzens Hoy,
> *Critical Resistance: From Poststructuralism to Postcritique* (2004)

each case judged independently of a moral schema. David Couzens Hoy, professor of philosophy at the University of California, Santa Cruz, has identified an "ethical turn" in philosophy in the 1980s and 1990s. He describes modern ethics as "obligations that present themselves as necessarily to be fulfilled but are neither forced on one or are enforceable". He sees acts such as rejecting consumerism in favour of simpler

Burmese politician Aung San Suu Kyi has campaigned for peaceful change in Burma for decades, preferring ethical resistance to violent struggle.

ways of living, or boycotting businesses that avoid paying tax, as examples of "ethical resistance" – a way for the powerless to push back against the powerful.

The powerless can be any group, human or not, including the poor, the unborn, animals and marginalized ethnic or sexual groups.

The good life

The consensus of the last two millennia seems to be that living a good, morally virtuous life is likely to produce happiness. This will not produce material wealth – indeed, in many cases selfish and immoral behavior has a better chance of producing more material wealth – but it will at least enable us, as individuals, to feel true to ourselves, free from guilt, shame and fear of exposure. Living virtuously is not dependent on religion. Although religion may offer people a pre-prepared moral code, a blueprint for virtuous living, and the religious often claim a monopoly on morality, the drive to goodness is in all – or most – of us. Living well is, in Aristotle's terms, the way to become a fully realized human, fulfilling one's natural purpose. But living well is not something that can be done in isolation – we can't all be Diogenes. So truly living well involves relating to other people in a moral and virtuous manner – enacting virtue in our political and social structures.

CHAPTER 6

How do we make a
GOOD
SOCIETY?

*"I am not an Athenian or a Corinthian,
but a citizen of the world."*

Diogenes of Sinope
(according to Epictetus, *Discourses*)

*"That to secure these Rights,
Governments are instituted among Men . . .
Whenever any Form of Government becomes
destructive of these Ends, it is the Right of
the People to alter or to abolish it."*

Thomas Jefferson,
United States Declaration of Independence
(1776)

A good society allows its people freedom to protest.

The two basic philosophical questions of "how do you live a good life?" and "how do you make a good society?" are inextricably linked, as we all have to live with other people. Ethics should underpin any legal and political system, but there are other considerations, too. By extending what is "right"

> **IS THE WHOLE OTHER THAN THE SUM OF ITS PARTS?**
> There are, broadly speaking, two approaches to political philosophy. The individualist approach sees societies as the sum of the individuals within them. The other, collectivist, approach sees a society as more than a collection of people, but as something that has its own autonomy and identity. The importance of individuals is lessened in the collectivist view.

to a whole society, some compromises must inevitably be made. The criticism levelled at Diogenes, that the ascetic way he believed we should live could not be sustained by a whole society, goes to the heart of the dilemma. We can't all eschew material goods and we can't all have less (or more) than everyone else.

The ethical citizen in an ethical society

Philosophers have differed in their view of the degree to which ethics should dictate policy or the legal code. The Italian politician and diplomat Niccolò Machiavelli (1469–1527) spared no time for morality. His entirely pragmatic approach is the opposite of Bentham's proposed revision of the legal code along ethical grounds. But there are other considerations, too. Who should set out the law, and how should it be enforced? What gives a government legitimacy? What form should a government take? What are the obligations of a government towards its citizens and what duties do citizens owe to it? And finally, is it ever right to overthrow a government?

In some ways, political philosophy is the practical application of metaphysics. It involves defining concepts such as justice, freedom, authority and fairness and then finding social structures in which they can be implemented.

The social contract

The idea that there is a social contract between the individual and society first surfaces in Plato's work and persists to the present day. In Plato's *Crito*, the character of Socrates says that he has entered into a contract with the city of Athens by staying in it after maturity, and as

The Prince, by Niccolò Machiavelli (left), has been used as a reference manual by many political leaders, including Joseph Stalin.

THE FOUR OPTIONS

There are four broadly distinct political positions:

Liberalism – inclines towards equality and freedom for all, but the inherent problem of people being personally unequal (in intelligence, for instance) leads to an equality of opportunity or resources being the best that can be achieved.

Conservatism – distrusts wholesale revision and believes that practices that don't work will slowly die out on their own. Conservatism trusts everything to find its own level, including the market – hence an adherence to free-market capitalism.

Socialism – believes that resources are better used and managed if owned collectively so that individual bias or ambition cannot operate to the detriment of the whole of society. There may be moral or practical reasons for approving of state ownership.

Anarchism – holds that people cannot live a good life, which is different for different individuals, if they are constrained by a hierarchy or set of limitations. The difficulty for anarchy is in recognizing which structures are naturally emerging (and may form part of a good life) and which are imposed.

part of that contract he is bound by the city's laws and by its judgement of him. As a consequence of entering into that contract, he must accept the punishment of execution, even if he feels it was handed down unjustly.

The good of the state

Plato's *Republic* is the first substantial work of political philosophy. It describes a utopian society led by an elite class of guardians who are trained from birth to rule. The rest of society is divided into soldiers and the common people. In the republic, the ideal citizens are those who understand how best to use their talents to benefit society, and do precisely what is needed to achieve that. Everything is organized for the good of the state as a whole, with little regard for personal freedom or individual rights. Such a society, Plato believed, would be just to all its citizens, giving to and taking from each

as is their due. It would also be invincible as its structure would make it so much stronger than any of its enemies.

The Republic extends Plato's idea of "Forms" to the realm of politics. It describes the ideal society of which all real societies are only imperfect approximations or copies. No existing society (in Plato's time or now) manages to promote the good of all citizens, a feature of the ideal.

The vision of society portrayed in *The Republic* has been criticized extensively over the last 2,300 years. The British philosopher Bertrand Russell (1872–1970), with the benefit of considerable hindsight and historical perspective, accused Plato of endorsing an elitist and totalitarian regime under the guise of communist or socialist principles. After the spectacular failure of a series of communist and fascist totalitarian states during the 20th century, the ideal looks as if it might be in need of a rethink.

The constitution as soul

Plato's pupil Aristotle severely criticized *The Republic*. Employed by Philip II of Macedon as personal tutor to the boy who would become Alexander the Great, Aristotle had seen high-level politics at first hand. His *Politics* gives advice to rulers and statesmen based on his view that the role of political leaders is to frame the laws or constitution, then maintain and revise them as necessary. He believed that the natural function of man is to act according to reason based in virtue, and this should be both harnessed and recognized in political structures.

He thought that the constitution is to the city-state the equivalent of a soul in a living organism. The city-state is a compound of a particular population, in a specific territory with a constitution that defines the aim of the city-state. The aim of the properly constituted city-state is the happiness of the citizens. His *Politics* discusses the ideal city-state, and classifies and discusses the merits and demerits of various types of government.

> **PHILOSOPHERSPEAK: UTOPIA**
>
> "Utopia" has become a generic term for an ideal, imaginary state with a perfect constitution and society.

Aristotle considered that humans naturally come together to form societies (a doctrine called political naturalism) and that humans are political animals. His definition of a "citizen", though, is rather narrow, excluding women, slaves, children and foreigners. The remainder are full citizens in that they play a part in the running of the city-state.

His analysis of the different forms of government divided them into just (correct) and unjust (deviant) forms, adapted from Plato (*see* table opposite):

Although he considered a ruler who exerts absolute power over citizens to be a tyrant, Aristotle saw no problem with exerting absolute power over slaves, women or children: he considered women and children to be of reduced rational capacity and in need of guidance, and "natural" slaves lacking direction and needing a master.

Justice, according to Aristotle, requires that individuals receive benefits in proportion to their merit or deserts. The city-state is neither a business enterprise to maximize wealth (as the oligarchs suppose) nor an association to promote

The flipside of the freedom to flourish is the freedom to starve. How can a society provide the first while guarding against the second?

Ancient Greek laws inscribed on stone plinths are evidence of a determination to set society on a firm and formal footing with rules that can be referred to in order to sort out disputes.

liberty and equality (as the democrats maintain). Instead, its aim is "the good life", which is a life consisting of noble actions. The ideal constitution is one in which the citizens are fully virtuous.

Aristotle criticized Plato's *Republic* for being too concerned with the city-state rather than the individual citizens, and for promoting an approach that is counter to human nature. His own recommendations were more pragmatic. Although he discussed an ideal constitution, he acknowledged that most lawgivers won't be in a position to institute the ideal but will have to make compromises.

In practical terms, the best government often turns out to be government by the many. Although Aristotle considered democracy a bad thing, government by the middle classes is, he believed, often better than government by a few rich people. Both the rich and the poor are inclined to make bad decisions on account of their personal feelings and interests, while the middle classes will be more moderate. The idea that if many citizens with some individual merits govern together their collective merits will benefit society underpins many modern constitutions.

	CORRECT	DEVIANT
ONE RULER	Kingship	Tyranny
FEW RULERS	Aristocracy	Oligarchy
MANY RULERS	Polity	Democracy

'since we see that every city-state is a sort of community and that every community is established for the sake of some good (for everyone does everything for the sake of what they believe to be good), it is clear that every community aims at some good, and the community which has the most authority of all and includes all the others aims highest, that is, at the good with the most authority. This is what is called the city-state or political community."

Aristotle, *Politics*

Marcus Aurelius was both a Stoic philosopher and Roman Emperor. He was co-emperor with Lucius Verus from 161–169 and ruled alone from 169–180.

Aristotle covered in depth many of the enduring concerns of political philosophy: the role of human nature, ideals and morality in practical politics; the relation of the individual to the state; the theory of justice; the rule of law; constitutions; and the causes of revolution.

Glimmers of equality

We might be inclined to let Aristotle off the hook for his view about slaves and women just because of the time he lived in. But the job of a philosopher is to expose everything to scrutiny. Seneca, writing in Rome (a place also rather fond of slave-ownership), managed to set aside the common view when he wrote, around CE65:

"Kindly remember that he whom you call your slave sprang from the same stock, is smiled upon by the same skies, and on equal terms with yourself breathes, lives, and dies."

The Stoics held that external differences between people are of no consequence and all people are naturally born equal. Of course, a belief that all people are equal is not

> "Freedom is secured not by the fulfilling of men's desires, but by the removal of desire."
>
> Epictetus (CE55–135)

very convenient for rulers, and disappeared from political philosophy for a long time.

A convert to Stoicism, the Roman emperor Marcus Aurelius (CE121–180) was something of a personal contradiction. Although in his *Meditations* he showed concern for the social problems of the poor, slaves, and the imprisoned, as emperor he continued to persecute the Christian population. The *Meditations* are a collection of aphorisms that present his ideas on ethics and politics. They are not supported by debate, reasoning or analysis. In one sense, Stoicism was quite a convenient belief system for a ruler to espouse, as it encouraged people to accept things as they are and look inwards for satisfaction. According to the Stoics, all "ensouled beings" strive towards self-preservation, which means looking for what is in tune with its nature. In mankind, that which is going to be good at all times is virtue.

Bringing God to the city

St Augustine was born and died in North Africa, though he spent some time in Rome and Milan. A convert to Christianity in his early thirties, he devoted himself to trying to show that reason upheld faith.

While Augustine tried to reconcile Christian thinking with the writings of Plato (filtered through the neoplatonists), and Thomas Aquinas did the same for Aristotle, medieval Christian philosophers paid little attention to the issue of politics independently of this legacy. There was a tendency to dismiss politics as not really the business of the Christian. Rendering unto Caesar that which is Caesar's seems to have included temporal power and political concerns. Augustine wrote that the Christian community was a spiritual community and not a political community. Aquinas, writing 800 years later, identified four levels of law, with God's divine law at the top and temporal human law at the bottom – still not of great interest. It was not until the Renaissance, with its turmoil and intellectual advances, that political theory re-emerged as a concern of philosophers.

The devil you know . . .

Born in Florence at the time of devious machinations of the great political Italian families, Niccolò Machiavelli was the most influential political philosopher of the Renaissance. His greatest work, *The Prince* (1532), was presented as a guide to rulers, giving a detailed analysis of successful political techniques. The text is amoral rather than immoral, and the popular characterization of Machiavelli as evil and conniving is unjust. The belief that the nickname "Old Nick" comes from Machiavelli's name is probably wrong – but it does demonstrate the reputation he has had.

Machiavelli's advice to princes is entirely practical and gives barely a thought to the morality of the methods. In his view, the ends justify the means as long as the ends

THE "JUST WAR" PROBLEM

A problem in political philosophy that has been of recent interest in the West is that of the "just war". The problem was introduced by St Augustine in his work on Christian philosophy, *The City of God*. Plato had said simply that "justice is in the interest of the stronger", a simple statement of "right is might". Augustine divided the issue into two questions: "Is it right to go to war?" and "What actions are allowable in a war?" He required that four main conditions be met for a war to be considered moral:

1. Just Authority – the decision to go to war must be based on a legitimate political and legal process.

2. Just Cause – war is the most appropriate response to a wrong that has been committed.

3. Right Intention – the war action is limited to righting the wrong (no "mission creep" is allowed).

4. Last Resort – other avenues have been explored and war is the only remaining option.

There are then moral limits on what is allowed in a war that has passed the first set of criteria. An army must only use force in proportion to the cause and must not do more than is necessary to correct the wrong suffered. An army must not attack innocent, non-combatant civilians. An army is not responsible for unforeseen bad consequences as long as the good of war outweighs the bad and the war was carried out with good intentions.

Augustine came up with his guidelines at a time when the Roman Empire was in decline and was falling to other powers. The question of the morality of war was of immediate and urgent importance – as it has remained.

are worthwhile – and that remains true pretty much regardless of what means are employed to attain them. But the ends should be politically "good" – goals that are worth achieving. The three goals Machiavelli thinks the effective prince should strive for are national security, independence, and a strong constitution. There is no point trying to pursue these without sufficient resources, though, as failure will be inevitable. He advises princes to follow their convictions with strength and courage, doing whatever is necessary.

Most of the practical advice relates to manipulating people – supporters, allies, the populace and other rulers – in order to attain and retain power. He noted that it is often useful to appear virtuous in order to win support. To be an outright tyrant is generally a bad move as it is antagonistic and makes ruling more difficult and the prince's position insecure. A prince needs to aim for a reasonably content population as they will be easy to govern and not keen to overthrow him, and for that reason only it is sensible to deal fairly, if firmly, with the populace. The most successful form of government, he says in his *Discourses* (*c*.1517), is a republic run by princes, but held in check by the nobility and ordinary citizens.

Protesters against the war in Iraq. According to St Augustine, a just war must have a just cause and must be the only appropriate response; war must be entered into only after due legal process and actions must be limited to righting wrongs suffered.

Perfect worlds

Several philosophers have followed Plato in setting out their blueprint for a perfect society by describing a utopia – an ideal state. The social philosopher and statesman Sir Thomas More (1478–1535) called his visionary land "Utopia" (from the Greek *eu-topos*, meaning "good place") and described it in a book of the same name. For a long time, More was a trusted adviser to Henry VIII. He was too principled and honest to last; Henry had him executed in 1535 when More, a devout Catholic, would not endorse Henry's divorce, remarriage and appointment as the head of the new Church of England.

Utopia (1516) is presented as a dialogue, with a traveller, Raphael Hythloday, describing the island of Utopia in the South Seas. Hythloday has just returned after living there for five years. Utopia is essentially a communist state; no one is allowed to keep personal property, there is no personal ambition or commerce (except with other lands). Nearly everyone is equal. The exceptions are the bondsmen who carry out the most unpleasant tasks. These are either criminals or foreigners under sentence of death. Everyone works six days a week, wears the same clothes and lives in identical houses, which they have to swap regularly to discourage the residents from customizing them or becoming too attached to them. The towns are all built to a regular plan, people eat communally and everyone has everything they need.

One way in which Utopia is very different from the oppressive communist regimes of the 20th century is in its religious tolerance: all religions are tolerated, but not atheism. More held that if someone did not believe in God, they could not be trusted to recognize any other authority and so would not be a governable citizen.

> "Life in More's Utopia, as in most others, would be intolerably dull. Diversity is essential to happiness, and in Utopia there is hardly any."
>
> Bertrand Russell

Humanist Sir Thomas More (considered a saint by the Catholic Church) was executed for opposing Henry VIII.

Intellectuals and governors are chosen on merit in Utopia and stay in post only for as long as they are good at what they are supposed to be doing. They can't inherit the position or continue in it if indigent or lazy. The head of state is an elected prince who can be removed if he turns out to be a tyrant.

Utopia gave More a way of depicting an alternative view of society without openly criticizing Henry VIII's England. He used the book to articulate socialist ideals completely unfamiliar and unvoiced in Tudor England. Whether More believed Utopia depicted a possible or even desirable society is not clear, but many other authors took their cue from him and wrote about imaginary societies. Indeed, Shakespeare's late play *The Tempest* (1623) tackles a similar theme, with the magician Prospero trying (but failing) to make an isolated island paradise for himself and his daughter.

Natural man and natural law

During the 17th and 18th centuries, several very influential philosophical thinkers turned their attention to the nature of society and the type of social contract humankind makes in order to form them. One of Aquinas" four levels of law was "natural law" – rules that result pretty much from the application of reason. The idea of natural law and how humans would behave in a "natural" state became a focus of interest for several political philosophers. They had very different ideas about what constituted a "natural" (non-civic) state as this was a condition that was almost impossible to witness at first hand. Travellers" tales of native peoples inhabiting newly discovered lands such as the Americas or Australia fed information of dubious reliability into the debate.

The laws of the universe applied to society

The English philosopher Thomas Hobbes (1596–1650) sought a new methodology to underpin his political philosophy. Like Descartes, he looked to the developments in science for a model: if, as Galileo and Newton had demonstrated, the universe worked according to a set of natural rules, why shouldn't this also be the case for social structures? So Hobbes applied the rule of natural law to the realm of politics. His first treatise on political science, *Elements of Law*, was distributed to supporters of King Charles I in 1640 to justify the king's actions to an increasingly hostile parliament. Hobbes spent the next ten years in self-imposed exile in France. There, he first developed his defence of a king's right to rule as an absolute monarch in *De Cive* (1642). He revisited the topic at length in his masterpiece, *Leviathan* (1651).

Despite Hobbes" best efforts, the British public was not convinced of the merits of putting themselves in the hands of the monarch and Charles I was executed in 1649.

Leviathan starts with the assumption that all people naturally seek their own personal good and that if this instinct is left unchecked, social chaos will result. To prevent having to fight all the time, people willingly surrender their individual rights to the authority of a ruler, which Hobbes calls a sovereign (though that might be either a monarch or a governing assembly). In return, the sovereign ensures the well-being and security of the people. Put another way, the natural state of humankind is one of war and strife, and only the rules of social living, imposed by force, prevent us from falling back into that natural state. Without the covenant between individuals and the sovereign, Hobbes says, society would disintegrate and it would be "a war of every man, against every man" and everyone's life would be "solitary, poor, nasty, brutish and short".

The social contract prevents humankind from reverting to this state and it works because it offers safety and sufficient of what we need – so although every individual is still self-interested, each person's needs are met in a way that takes account of everyone else's needs.

Not all bad

John Locke took a more benevolent view of humanity. While he still believed that human nature encourages us to be selfish, he regarded it as being characterized by reason and tolerance. He considered that in their "natural state", individuals had a right to protect their "life, health, liberty, or possessions". They first drew together

Explorers reporting on humans in their "natural" state variously characterized them as either noble savages or degraded subhumans: philosophers could take their pick.

to resolve conflicts and defend rights in a civil way, quickly finding it easier to defend such rights as a group. He saw the creation and accumulation of property as initially limited: people had to work to produce goods, which were generally perishable.

The introduction of money then enabled people to keep producing and swapping perishable goods for something that endures and retains its value, so removing the limit on accumulation. He believed in market forces, saying that the value of anything will rise and fall according to how much is available and how many people want it (supply and demand).

He saw money as a good thing, since it could prevent waste, and he considered unused property to be a waste and an offence against nature. Locke believed that social inequality was a result of the tacit agreement that societies make about how to use money. He recognized that it was the job of governments to introduce rules that would moderate the conflict between unlimited accumulation and equal distribution, but he didn't consider it his task to think about how this might be done.

Locke supported a constitutional monarchy as the ideal form of government but denied the divine right of kings – that a king is given his position by God and so may not be overthrown. In *Two Treatises of Government* (1690) he argued against hereditary power and an absolute monarchy, claiming that a government is only legitimate if the rulers rule with the consent of the citizens. He believed that both parts of the social contract must be upheld: the people must obey the rulers, but the rulers have a duty to support and nurture the citizens.

Thomas Hobbes took a dim view of humankind, believing that left to our own devices with no social structure we would resort to selfish and destructive behaviour.

The noble savage

Jean-Jacques Rousseau took a much rosier view of humankind's natural state. Instead of constantly bickering and knifing one another in the back for the last biscuit, as Hobbes believed would be our normal behavior, Rousseau considered the natural state of humans to be innately good:

"Men in a state of nature do not know good and evil, but only their independence."

This natural knowledge, along with "the peacefulness of their passions, and their ignorance of vice, prevents them from doing ill".

It was a sublimely optimistic approach, and one that laid all the ills of humankind at the door of the social structures we have

173

built. The entire Romantic movement, in philosophy, art, literature and music, stems from Rousseau's belief that the innate state of humankind is one of nobility and natural grandeur and that the closer we can be to our nature (and to Nature) the better we will live.

Rousseau set out his ideas for creating a perfect society in *The Social Contract* (1762), probably the most influential and outstanding work of political philosophy of the 18th century. It was a natural successor to his earlier work, *The Discourse on Inequality* (1754), in which he criticized the injustice he witnessed everywhere in the world around him. He saw this injustice as the direct result of educational and social structures that suppressed the natural will and ability of men.

In the famous opening line of *The Social Contract* (*see* box above), Rousseau set out his premise that society robs humankind of nobility and natural freedom. Yet he goes on to say that it is the social contract – the covenant between individuals agreeing to be governed – that renders us free. The freedom that the solitary human enjoys is the freedom to pursue personal wellbeing without comparison or harmful consideration of others. Society, with its trappings of wealth and ambition, removes this freedom. We become concerned with what others have, with our position in relation to others, and so become dissatisfied, acquisitive, envious and cruel. Instead of a natural impulse to attain what we need – food, shelter, a mate – we strive for unnecessary things that society has taught us to want. This result has come

> *"Man was born free, and he is everywhere in chains. Those who think themselves the masters of others are indeed greater slaves than they."*
> Jean-Jacques Rousseau, *The Social Contract* (1762)

about because the societies we have built (it holds true now, as well as in 18th-century France) have a faulty social contract. People have been coerced into giving up their natural freedoms in exchange for a kind of slavery in a society designed by and for the rich.

A good society, according to Rousseau, is based on principles of classical republicanism. The people come together and govern in a democracy that sets laws that are for the benefit of society as a whole. As the laws are an expression of general will, it is in each person's interests to obey these laws and doing so is in fact both an expression and attainment of freedom.

> *"The first man who, having fenced in a piece of land, said, "This is mine," and found people naïve enough to believe him, that man was the true founder of civil society. From how many crimes, wars, and murders, from how many horrors and misfortunes might not any one have saved mankind, by pulling up the stakes, or filling up the ditch, and crying to his fellows: Beware of listening to this impostor; you are undone if you once forget that the fruits of the earth belong to us all, and the earth itself to nobody."*
> Jean-Jacques Rousseau, *Discourse on Inequality* (1754)

JEAN-JACQUES ROUSSEAU (1712–78)

Rousseau, the son of a watchmaker, was born in Geneva. His mother died in childbirth and his father abandoned him when he fled Geneva to escape impending legal difficulties. At the age of 15, Rousseau left Geneva too and wandered from place to place, finally being taken in by Françoise-Louise de Warens, a 29-year-old noblewoman who was being paid by the King of Piedmont to convert Protestants to Catholicism. Rousseau became her lover when he was 20 years old. He published his first book when he was nearly 40, and rapidly became famous.

Despite writing an almost modern treatise on education and how to raise children, Rousseau was not an ideal family man himself. He fathered a number of children with Thérèse Levasseur, his lover in Paris, before marrying her and he insisted she take several of them to the foundling hospital. He later tried to trace his son but failed. His views on equality did not extend to women, whom he believed should be ruled in the home by their husbands.

Although he became the leading French philosopher of the Enlightenment, Rousseau fell out with almost everyone who knew him, including Madame de Warens, his friend the philosopher David Hume, the Catholics, the Protestants and the Government of France. After fleeing from one country after another, he ended up near Paris, where he died, probably of a brain haemorrhage. Sixteen years after his death, his body was reburied in the Panthéon in Paris.

This led to the apparently paradoxical and chilling assertion by Rousseau that people must be "forced to be free": in other words, made to obey the laws that exist to make people free through partaking in the social contract.

The general will takes absolute precedence over individual wills, and Rousseau even goes so far as to deny individual rights and say that any notion of them must be given up. These should not be necessary in the properly constituted society,

as what is good-for-all is necessarily good-for-one. This all looks hopelessly optimistic, and there are of course many cases in which what is good for the many does not look at all good for every individual. Rousseau recognized that people don't necessarily know what is good for them, and explained that when they don't know their "real will" they need a great legislator to reveal it to them.

Staunch Victorian Conservatives resisted calls for social reform because Conservatism believes that wrongs will right themselves with time. But at what human cost?

Trusting the general will

The general will is more than just the sum of all the individual wills. It is the will of all directed towards their communal, rather than individual, good:

"Each of us puts his person and all his power in common under the supreme direction of the general will, and, in our corporate capacity, we receive each member as an indivisible part of the whole."

The general will takes on something of the character of an autonomous entity. This stops the exploitation or neglect of minority groups. For instance, it would benefit the majority of people in a country where most people don't have red hair to confiscate the goods of red-haired people and redistribute them among non-red-haired people. That would prioritize the majority will (the wills of the majority of individuals) over the common will. The will of the individuals who make up society is to enhance their personal wealth. But the general will is to create an equitable and sustainable society with minimal conflict and injustice. The majority will is served by confiscating and redistributing the property of red-haired people, but the general will is served by letting red-haired people own property on the same terms as everyone else.

Rousseau regarded the ruler as the agent of the people, not their master. Yet, in saying that he believed everyone must follow what is deemed to be the general good as set out by the ruler, he has sometimes been accused of licensing totalitarianism and tyranny. But he argued that as the sovereign can only impose rules in the name of the general will – that is, what is good for all – the sovereign can't be a despot as there is no disjunction between what the sovereign ordains and the interests of his people.

Rousseau insisted that his social plan

"Forced to be free": punishing those who don't comply with laws set out for the general good is, in Rousseau's terms, forcing them to be free.

will really only work in small city-states such as those of Ancient Greece. This is a problem in a world comprising large nation-states and even empires. At the end of *The Social Contract*, Rousseau asks, "What is to be done?" The answer he gives is that everyone must cultivate their personal virtues and obey the rule of law. The answer the French people gave, and rulers around Europe feared, was to overthrow the rule of law in the hope of instituting something better.

The individual will to own extravagant, fuel-hungry vehicles is in conflict with the general will to protect the environment.

Revolution!

One of the key questions in political philosophy is under what circumstances a ruler can legitimately be overthrown. Aristotle made the point that a tyrant is not acting like a ruler and so surrenders the right to rule. This view was taken up by Aquinas and carried on into the Middle Ages. Machiavelli concentrated on helping the ruler to stay the right side of tyranny so that the people would not revolt. The true philosophers of revolt, though, came to the fore in the 18th century – and revolutions followed.

Opinion polls in the UK repeatedly call for a return to capital punishment, abolished in the last century and now illegal under EU charter – an example of the people not knowing their "real will"?

THE FRENCH REVOLUTION

The French Revolution was the bloodiest revolution of the 18th and 19th centuries. The extravagant lifestyles of the aristocracy, Enlightenment ideas about equality and freedom, and fiscal problems in France all fueled unrest among the common people. In 1789, the starving peasantry and urban poor rose up against the ruling classes and revolution ensued, beginning with the storming of the Bastille prison in Paris in July. In 1792, a Republic was declared and King Louis XVI was executed the following year.

Struggles and dissent between the revolutionaries marked the whole period. During 1793 and 1794, Maximilien Robespierre leader of the Jacobins, headed the so-called Reign of Terror in which up to 40,000 people were killed, many executed by guillotine. The Jacobins fell in 1795 and the Directory took control of France until the Consulate took over in 1799 with Napoleon Bonaparte in charge.

> *"A statue of gold should be erected to you in every city in the universe."*
> Emperor Napoleon Bonaparte of France, talking to Thomas Paine

In this cartoon by James Gillray, Paine has a nightmare in which three judges carry scrolls listing charges and punishments.

Very common sense

In 1774, the English-born political philosopher Thomas Paine (1737–1809) emigrated to America, where he wrote for and later edited the *Pennsylvania Magazine* and published one of the first essays calling for the abolition of slavery. At the start of the American War of Independence in 1776, Paine anonymously published a pamphlet titled *Common Sense* in support of the revolution. It recommended that America throw off its British colonial overlords and become self-governing. As well as detailing Paine's objections to a constitutional monarchy, the pamphlet proposed a method of democratic government. Paine argued against any hereditary office or aristocracy, and said that government and social status must be kept separate. He claimed that independence for the American colonies was justified morally – and also practically, as they could be self-supporting.

After the success of the War of Independence, Paine went first to France and then to England. Responding to Edmund Burke's *Reflections on the Revolution in France* (1790), Paine produced his seminal treatise on democracy, *The Rights of Man*, in 1791. In this he asserted that all men are born with equal rights, but living socially we can't always either defend our rights or avoid violating the rights of others. By establishing a state and a constitution, we can encode our rights as civil rights that can be defended and enforced on our behalf. In Paine's view, the only morally acceptable form of government is a democratic republic in which citizens vote to choose their leaders. England and France, he claimed, had immoral constitutions as this right was denied the citizens. This was sufficient justification for the populations of England and France to overthrow their governments, he claimed.

> *"The completest charlatan that ever existed."*
> Thomas Paine, commenting on Emperor Napoleon Bonaparte

The British Government immediately charged Paine with treason and, once he had fled to France, quashed the incipient British revolution. Paine was welcomed in France and given a seat in the National Convention, but France was still in a

EDMUND BURKE, *REFLECTIONS ON THE REVOLUTION IN FRANCE* **(1790)**

The Irish statesman and philosopher Edmund Burke (1729–97) declared that the French Revolution would fail disastrously as its foundations took no account of human nature. He spoke against Enlightenment and the ideas of Hobbes, saying that society should be handled like a living organism – infinitely complex and requiring compassionate engagement – and should not be reduced to a set of rules. He promoted slow constitutional change to introduce specific rights and liberties rather than radical overthrow by means of a revolution in the name of abstract Rights and Liberty. With considerable prescience, he predicted that the revolution in France would lead to squabbling factions until eventually one general would emerge as leader and edge towards tyranny.

volatile state and he was later imprisoned on Robespierre's orders. He escaped execution only because of Robespierre's own downfall, which came shortly after Paine's arrest. Paine returned to America in 1802, but his rejection of organized religion and of the idea of a vengeful God made him deeply unpopular in profoundly Christian America, and he died in obscurity.

The "hyena in petticoats"

Thinking along the same lines as Thomas Paine, Mary Wollstonecraft (1759–97) was one of the few influential female philosophers to have lived before the 20th century. She could have given a good account of why so few women became philosophers. Most famous for her *Vindication of the Rights of Woman* (1792), the text that arguably

Burke predicted that a "popular general" would emerge as "master of [the French revolutionary] assembly, the master of [the] whole republic." Napoleon came to power in 1799 and was declared emperor in 1804.

Three hundred years ahead of his time, Paine argued that there should be a tax on inherited wealth and it should be used to provide a welfare system to help those in need.

initiated the feminist movement, she was a political philosopher of considerable talent. She wrote first about the rights of men.

Responding to Burke's *Reflections on the French Revolution*, her *Vindication of the Rights of Men* argued that the populace has the right to remove a bad king, and that slavery and contemporary treatment of the poor were immoral. She called for the dissolution of the monarchy and an end to the power of the Church, both of which she considered oppressive. She saw education as the focus for reform: the educational practices of the time, she said, did not equip women to participate as citizens and make use of their abilities, but only to be decorative servants to men. She deplored the way women (and men) paid attention only to how women look and encouraged other women to be docile and enter into marriages that are effectively "legal prostitution":

"I have turned over various books written on the subject of education, and patiently observed the conduct of parents and the management of schools; but what has been the result? A profound conviction that the neglected education of my fellow-creatures is the grand source of the misery I deplore."

Wollstonecraft was adamant that the subjugation of women is harmful to men as well as to women, as it reduces the portion of reason, knowledge and virtue available to benefit society as a whole. Bad treatment of women, she argued, encourages them to be sly, debases them, creates discord in the home and perpetuates the wrong values by passing them on to their children. She claimed, too, that if women were not given rights, they also could not be shouldered with responsibilities; rights come with duties, and we can't have one without the other.

Had Wollstonecraft not died at the age of 38, just ten days after giving birth to her daughter, feminist philosophy might have progressed a lot more quickly than it did. The daughter survived – she was Mary Wollstonecraft Shelley, author of *Frankenstein* (1823).

Social mathematics

Despite Burke's plea for heart-based government, the end of the 18th century saw a move towards an almost mechanically mathematical approach to society and law-

"The civilized women of the present century, with a few exceptions, are only anxious to inspire love, when they ought to cherish a nobler ambition, and by their abilities and virtues exact respect."

Mary Wollstonecraft, *Vindication of the Rights of Woman* (1792)

Mary Wollstonecraft was the first significant female philosopher of the modern era.

THE SPIRIT OF THE LAWS

In 1748, the French political philosopher Charles de Secondat, Baron de Montesquieu analysed political structures and isolated three, each driven by a spirit or "spring":

▶ For democratic and aristocratic republics, the spring is the love of virtue – the willingness to put the interests of the community ahead of private interests. (An aristocratic republic is one in which power is restricted to a few, such as the noble families who were allowed a vote in the Venetian Republic. A democratic republic allows everyone – or at least every male – a vote.)

▶ For monarchies, the spring is love of honor – the drive for rank and privilege.

▶ For despotism, the spring is fear.

If the spring is not powerful enough to sustain the social order, the political system will collapse. Montesquieu said that the English did not manage to retain a republic under Cromwell because they had insufficient love of virtue.

building. Both the seminal capitalist text and the development of utilitarianism belong to this period.

The math of money

At exactly the same time that Paine was stirring up revolution with his pamphlet *Common Sense*, the Scottish moral philosopher Adam Smith (1723–90) was taking the opposite view and propping up the status quo with a justification of the inequalities in the political system. Known now as the economic theorist favoured by British prime minister Margaret Thatcher, Smith published the seminal treatise on capitalism, *An Inquiry into the Nature and Causes of the Wealth of Nations*, in 1776.

He promoted a free-market economy and had a firm belief that the "unintended consequences of intended action" benefit society. By this he meant that in serving their own interests people unintentionally serve the interests of society as a whole. For example, suppose a man decides to set up a business selling vegetables door to door. He does this because he wants to make a living and be his own boss. But there are unintentional benefits for other people: customers don't have to make their way to the shops or market; farmers benefit from him buying their produce; when his business expands and he employs others, he provides jobs in the community. In a free-market economy, these unintentional benefits only occur if a door-to-door vegetable service is genuinely good for the local community. If too few people want this service, his business will not succeed, or he will have to adapt it to suit the market conditions.

That all sounds very cosy, but it's easy to see where the problems are. People are going to consume a finite number of vegetables, and if they are buying from this man they are not buying from someone else, so other vegetable-sellers suffer a detrimental effect as a result of the competition. There is no simple solution.

Scottish economic theorist Adam Smith still exerts influence over fiscal policy 200 years after his death.

Smith's philosophy sets out no provision for the exploited losers in the free market – losers who were once in Western factories and farms, or in the slave plantations of the American south, but are now in the factories of emergent economic powers and the farms of South America, Africa and Asia. *The Wealth of Nations* remains one of the most important and influential works of economic and political philosophy in the history of Western thought.

Utility and utilitarianism

The belief that the "unintended consequences of intended action" will benefit society greatly influenced the industrial philanthropists of the 18th and 19th centuries, and the ideas of philosophers such as Jeremy Bentham. Bentham developed the principle of "utility" – the idea that humankind is motivated by the desire to seek pleasure and avoid pain. He applied this to political science, drawing up plans for a society and a legal code based on delivering the greatest good (pleasure) to the greatest number of people. In the *Introduction to the Principles of Morals and Legislation* (1789), the first document to outline utilitarianism, Bentham explained that legislation should try to harmonize the interests of society with those of private individuals pursuing their own happiness.

Bentham was a great reformer, and campaigned for many liberal causes. These included the abolition of slavery and all forms of physical punishment, the promotion of social equality for women, the decriminalization of consensual homosexuality, and an end to animal cruelty. Some of this was rather too pioneering for his time – his essay on homosexuality was not published until 1931.

Most famously, Bentham designed a prison called the "panopticon", in which prisoners would be visible to their guardians at all times (*see* panel on page 186). Being on view was supposed to encourage them to behave well, so it promoted the greatest good for the greatest number: if they behaved obediently, they would not be punished and so would not have to endure pain. Punishment was intended to reform the criminal and its extent was carefully calculated so that its long-term consequences would be a net increase in pleasure.

Putting morality on a very practical and quantitative footing, Bentham even devised an algorithm for calculating whether or not a proposed action or rule is good. He called it the "felicific calculus", and it involves a classification of 12 pains and 14 pleasures.

Smith's free-market philosophy produced the "unintended consequences" of extreme poverty and deprivation, exploitative working practices and lives of misery and degradation for the working-class urban poor of the Industrial Revolution.

> "The business of government is to promote the happiness of the society, by punishing and rewarding. . . . In proportion as an act tends to disturb that happiness, in proportion as the tendency of it is pernicious, will be the demand it creates for punishment."
>
> Jeremy Bentham, *An Introduction to the Principles of Morals and Legislation* (1789)

He described it in his *Introduction to the Principles of Morals and Legislation.* For each action, we need to consider the pleasures and pains that will result from it, taking account of their intensity, duration, certainty, propinquity (how soon the pleasure or pain will occur), fecundity (the chance that the sensation will be followed by more of the same type), purity (the chance that the sensation will be followed by the opposite type), and extent (how many people are

BENTHAM'S PANOPTICON

Bentham's design for a prison consisted of a ring of cells on several tiers arranged around a central watch-tower. The cells have glass fronts. The occupant of the watch-tower can see into all the cells, but the inmate of a cell can't see into the watch-tower. Michel Foucault described it as "a machine for dissociating the "see/being seen" dyad: in the peripheric ring, one is totally seen, without ever seeing; in the central tower, one sees everything without ever being seen." And a machine it was – a machine that delegated observation to the observed. Bentham designed it on the principle that surveillance should be "visible and unverifiable". The prisoners are aware that they could be watched at all times, but do not know when they are actually being watched. The effect is the same as if they were being watched all the time, as the prisoners become self-regulating in their behaviour.

FIG. III.—GROUND PLAN.

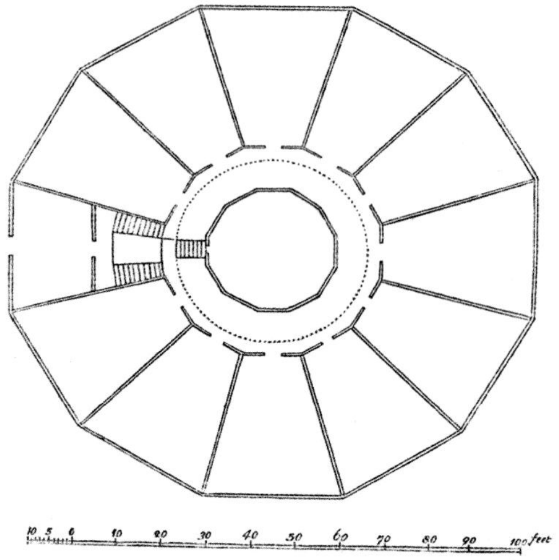

Trouble at t'mill

Bentham makes no distinction between happiness and pleasure, and treats pleasures and pain like countable beans that are directly and quantitatively comparable – both views with which his successor, John Stuart Mill, took issue. Like Rousseau, Bentham subordinated the good of the individual to the good of society in a way that, logically extended, could lead to the complete sacrifice of the one for the good of the many. It was a problem that Mill did not resolve in his

affected). Bentham wanted the calculator to be used in reforming criminal law. Using the calculator, it should have been possible to work out the minimum penalty to act as a deterrent to prevent any specific crime.

> *Bentham's "mnemonic doggerel" summed up "the whole fabric of morality and legislation":*
> *Intense, long, certain, speedy, fruitful, pure—*
> *Such marks in pleasures and in pains endure.*
> *Such pleasures seek if private be thy end:*
> *If it be public, wide let them extend.*
> *Such pains avoid, whichever be thy view:*
> *If pains must come, let them extend to few.*

The belief that being observed leads people to police their own behaviour has given us CCTV and speed cameras.

subsequent development of utilitarianism.

Mill agreed with Bentham that moral action should maximize pleasure and minimize pain and that this goal can guide us in choosing how to act.

Mill said that pleasure can't be reduced to a mere quantitative analysis without taking qualitative aspects into account. Not all pains and pleasures are equal – the pain of losing a pet is not the same as that of losing a parent – and even the way pain and pleasure are "rated" varies between individuals. Bentham's happiness calculator could not properly take account of these distinctions. Mill also insisted that some pleasures are of greater value than others. He felt that it was necessary to distinguish between "higher" and "lower" pleasures in the utilitarian calculation.

While Bentham had no particular interest in individual rights, Mill took a radical liberal view. It was not necessary, he felt, for us to scrutinize every tiny action of daily life and choose the option that created the greatest happiness for the largest number. Only when there are points of moral choice do we need to resort to

that method of deciding between actions. He stood up for the rights of the individual against the state, even if the government is democratically elected, speaking out for personal freedoms. In *On Liberty* (1859), Mill argued that "the only purpose for which power can be rightfully exercised over any member of a civilized community, against his will, is to prevent harm to others".

Modern utilitarians

The Australian moral philosopher Peter Singer (born 1946) is a modern-day utilitarianist, promoting what he calls "preference utilitarianism". While classical utilitarianism compares the morality of choice of actions by calculating which brings the greatest happiness to the most people, Singer decides the morality of an action by how far it satisfies desires and preferences. In making a judgement, we must look at the interests of all those involved and affected and choose the course that satisfies the most and frustrates the fewest desires and preferences. That all sounds fair enough, but Singer takes his argument to lengths that many consider extreme.

For Singer, life is not inherently worth while. We need to take account of quality of life, including a person's capacity to experience pleasure and self-fulfilment and to avoid suffering. In some cases, the conclusion might be that life is not worth living. He then endorses suicide, abortion, voluntary euthanasia and even involuntary euthanasia where the subject is unable to make a decision for physical reasons. He argues that seriously disabled infants could be killed up to the age of 28 days, as

> *"Nature has placed mankind under the governance of two sovereign masters, pain and pleasure. . . . They govern us in all we do, in all we say, in all we think: every effort we can make to throw off our subjection will serve but to demonstrate and confirm it. In words a man may pretend to abjure their empire, but in reality he will remain subject to it all the while."*
>
> Jeremy Bentham, *An Introduction to the Principles of Morals and Legislation* (1789)

there is no philosophical difference between aborting the unborn and killing a newborn. He would allow these killings if it were in the best interests of the afflicted individual and/or of the family.

But it's not all about harshness and slaughter. At the same time, he considers it morally indefensible that the rights afforded to humans should not also be afforded to animals, which are sentient beings capable of suffering pain. He rejects all cruelty to animals, including factory farming and animal experimentation, as manifestations of "speciesism" comparable with racism and sexism.

This is not because animals are inherently "equal" to humans (any more than all humans are equal in terms of their individual attributes) but that animals must be given equal consideration.

Singer's preference for utilitarianism could also be applied to the ethics of wealth distribution. He starts with the assumption that "suffering and death from lack of food, shelter, and medical care are bad", and argues that if we can prevent suffering and death in one place, without causing greater harm elsewhere, then we should do so. He uses the analogy of seeing a child drowning in a pond. If we saw a drowning child, we would rush into the pond to save the child, even at the expense of ruining our clothes and shoes: the loss of the clothes and shoes is a far lesser evil than the death of a child. The distance between ourselves and the sufferer is of no relevance, so if we are ever in a position to alleviate suffering, we should do so. It follows that if we would lose a pair of shoes to save a child drowning in a pond in front of us, then "if for the cost of a pair of shoes we can contribute to a health program in a developing country that stands a good chance of saving the life of a child, we ought to do so."

Towards communism

Many philosophers were intellectually involved in the French and American revolutions, commenting and encouraging on both sides, but two 19th-century German philosophers and social theorists were to have an even greater impact on politics. The

Mill's "greatest happiness" principle
"Actions are right in proportion as they tend to promote happiness, wrong as they tend to produce the reverse of happiness. By happiness is intended pleasure, and the absence of pain; by unhappiness, pain, and the privation of pleasure."

Dale Farm traveller site in the UK, which was cleared by bailiffs in 2011. Local residents often protest against proposals to build permanent sites for travellers. A utilitarian principle would say that the displeasure of the large local community outweighs the pleasure of the small number of travellers to be housed there. But the counter argument points out that extending such a principle would give the travellers nowhere to live.

two men, Karl Marx and Friedrich Engels, have perhaps done more to shape the world than any other political thinkers, for their writings were not just debated but taken up by revolutionaries and put into action.

Peter Singer's book Animal Liberation *(1975) argues that cruelty to animals is morally unjustifiable.*

Marx-und-Engels

Marx and Engels worked closely and are often spoken of together as a sort of composite philosopher, Marx-und-Engels (in German). Karl Marx is well known as the author of *Capital: Critique of Political Economy* (1867–93), better known as *Das Kapital*, and Engels for *The Condition of the Working Class in England* (1845). Together, Marx and Engels wrote *The Communist Manifesto* (1848). The philosophy underpinning their works is rooted in the ideas of Georg Hegel, who provided the notion of "dialectic". This is an approach to truth through an iterative process of proposing theses that are opposed by antitheses, leading to a synthesis that then becomes the new thesis. But whereas Hegel's dialectic was directed towards an absolute truth bound up in the divine, Marx-und-Engels favoured a "dialectical materialism" that had no recourse to God

> "If possessing a higher degree of intelligence does not entitle one human to use another for his own ends, how can it entitle humans to exploit nonhumans?"
>
> Peter Singer, *Animal Rights and Human Obligations* (1989)

and that dealt not with ideas but with actualities. This sounds more complex than it is: Marx-und-Engels simply meant that a repeating pattern of conflicts (in the form of class struggle) will lead inevitably to the "correct" social structure.

For Marx-und-Engels, the fundamental condition of humanity is the need to convert the raw material of the natural world into the goods necessary for survival. (For example, to dig metal from the ground and turn it into spoons, cars, and other useful objects.) As a result, the means of production, or the control of it, determines the shape of society:

"The hand-mill gives a society with the feudal lord; the steam-mill a society with the industrial capitalist."

Marx-und-Engels saw

What moral defence is there for not giving money to foreign aid programs?

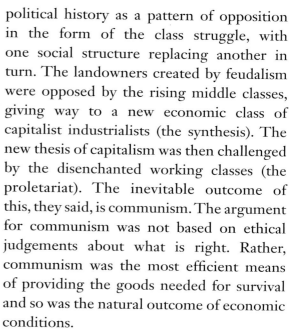

political history as a pattern of opposition in the form of the class struggle, with one social structure replacing another in turn. The landowners created by feudalism were opposed by the rising middle classes, giving way to a new economic class of capitalist industrialists (the synthesis). The new thesis of capitalism was then challenged by the disenchanted working classes (the proletariat). The inevitable outcome of this, they said, is communism. The argument for communism was not based on ethical judgements about what is right. Rather, communism was the most efficient means of providing the goods needed for survival and so was the natural outcome of economic conditions.

While Hegel saw changes in ideology and human understanding as being the drivers of social and political change, Marx-und-Engels saw economic and social change as leading to new ways of thinking. This is consistent with Marx's view of the relationship between the mind and the external world. He did not see the mind as a passive subject in an external world. He shared Kant's view that the mind is actively engaged with the objects of knowledge. But he went further than Kant, suggesting that both the mind and the world are continually adapting, and that we order our experience in ways that make it useful to our survival. For this reason, Marx didn't believe that social structures could be changed from the

> "The philosophers have only interpreted the world, the point is to change it."
>
> Karl Marx, *Theses on Feuerbach* (1845)

Karl Marx was born in Prussia in 1818, moved to Paris in 1843 but was exiled in 1849, spending the rest of his life in London.

top down – it was no use political thinkers coming up with ideas for reform. In Marx's view, society can only truly change from the bottom up – when the workers become aware of the oppressive situation they are in and rebel against it. Thinking will change only after society has changed. Consequently, Marx didn't feel it was possible to predict the form that communism would take – this could only be discovered after a social and economic revolution had taken place.

Unlike many of their contemporaries, Marx-und-Engels did not deplore the existence of the proletariat and look for ways of writing them out of the equation (as has largely happened with mechanization and computerization). Instead, they believed that the larger the proletariat, the sooner the revolution would come. The deplorable conditions that the proletariat were enduring would make them realize that change was necessary. This happened in both Russia and China in the 20th century, with disastrous consequences as untold millions died. It is too early to say what will be the result of the worsening state of the proletariat and the middle classes in the 21st century.

Counter-communism

The ruling capitalists were not keen on the idea that the workers could rise up and overthrow them. The work of the British economist John Maynard Keynes (1883–1946) seemed to offer a way of avoiding this happening. According to Keynesian economics, a downturn in the economy is a short-term problem resulting from a lack of demand. It can be solved by government increasing public spending to boost demand. Intervention by government could lead to a stable free-market economy that prevented the collapse of capitalism and the subsequent emergence

During the Russian Revolution in February 1917 the tsar's autocratic government was overthrown after an uprising by the workers.

Grand Duchesses Maria, Olga, Anastasia and Tatiana Nikolaevna of Russia in captivity, 1917. The Russian revolution overthrew the Romanovs and executed the whole family, leading to the foundation of a communist state.

of communism. This is the opposite of the approach advocated by Smith and Mill, who believed that if allowed to take its natural course the economic order will move towards the maximum wellbeing for both the individual and society.

Revolution taken to extremes

It is so difficult to find a social and political structure that is both fair and workable that some people

John Maynard Keynes recommended increased government spending as the way to lead an economy out of recession. Many European powers took the opposite approach in the 2010s.

have considered it impossible, and misguided to try, and would do away with all structures. The Russian revolutionary and thinker Mikhail Bakunin was the first true anarchist philosopher. He called for the overthrow of all styles of external authority, from God downwards, saying that people should be entirely self-governing:

"The liberty of man consists solely in this, that he obeys the laws of nature because he has himself recognized them as such, and not because they have been imposed upon him externally by any foreign will whatsoever, human or divine, collective or individual."

Mikhail Bakunin, *God and the State* (1871)

Bakunin developed a form of socialism called collective anarchism, in which the people would take possession of and manage the means of production, the land and everything else. They would have

---

THE CONDITION OF THE WORKING CLASS IN ENGLAND **(1845)**

The Russian communist revolutionary Vladimir Lenin (1874–1920) described Engels" book *The Condition of the Working Class in England* as "a terrible indictment of capitalism and the bourgeoisie . . . filled with the most authentic and shocking pictures of the misery of the English proletariat":

"What security has the working-man that it may not be his turn tomorrow? Who assures him employment, who vouches for it that, if for any reason or no reason his lord and master discharges him tomorrow, he can struggle along with those dependent upon him, until he may find someone else "to give him bread"? Who guarantees that willingness to work shall suffice to obtain work, that uprightness, industry, thrift, and the rest of the virtues recommended by the bourgeoisie, are really his road to happiness? No one. He knows that he has something today and that it does not depend upon himself whether he shall have something tomorrow."

Friedrich Engels

---

freedom of association and federation. Everyone, male or female, would have equal opportunities for education and equal means of subsistence and support. The peasants would "take the land and throw out those landlords who live by the labor of others". Unlike Marx, Bakunin did not exclude the *Lumpenproletariat* from his scheme – rather, the success of his project depended upon them, as they had the least attachment to the bourgeois scheme.

With some prescience, Bakunin saw that Marxism was not going to go well if implemented. Although he and Marx shared the same ultimate goal, Bakunin wanted it to be achieved by the proletariat rising up under their own steam and overthrowing all imposed social structures, while Marx wanted to act on behalf of the proletariat, creating a state that would, in theory, put their interests first. Bakunin objected:

"In reality, this would be for the proletariat a barrack-regime, under which the workingmen and the workingwomen, converted into a uniform mass, would rise, fall asleep, work, and live at the beat of the drum."

All totalitarian in the end

As many people have remarked, the communist revolution led in the end to totalitarian states that gave the workers no more freedom than right-wing totalitarian states. In both cases, the state as an entity in its own right took precedence over the individuals that comprised it. It is against this backdrop, of a world ravaged by the failure of totalitarianism, that the philosophers of the second half of the 20th century tried to piece together a more humane relationship between state and individual.

The American cognitive scientist and philosopher Noam Chomsky (born 1928) considers that there are only certain political structures we can successfully endure. Rejecting the idea that early experiences or conditioning determine what we will accept,

> ### PHILOSOPHERSPEAK: LUMPENPROLETARIAT
>
> The *Lumpenproletariat* are the lowest class of the masses, in Marx's definition. They include those who refuse to work and those who can't work through reasons of sickness and disability:
>
> "Vagabonds, discharged soldiers, discharged jailbirds, escaped galley slaves, swindlers, mountebanks, lazzaroni [street people], pickpockets, tricksters, gamblers, maquereaux [pimps], brothel keepers, porters, literati, organ grinders, ragpickers, knife grinders, tinkers, beggars — in short, the whole indefinite, disintegrated mass."
>
> Karl Marx, *The Eighteenth Brumaire of Louis Napoleon* (1852)

"No such thing as society"

In 1987, British prime minister Margaret Thatcher declared: "there is no such thing as society". Her words were an extreme extrapolation of the political philosophy of Robert Nozick (1938–2002). In 1974, the American philosopher argued for individual rights, following Kant's dictum: "Act so that you treat humanity, whether in your own person or in that of another, always as an end and never as a means only." He didn't interpret it quite how Kant had

he finds that a certain degree of free-ness (desire to be free to choose our actions and mode of life) is an innate feature of the human mind. Any political structure that tries to deny this or crush the individual is, ultimately, doomed to fail.

Keynesian economics would see government spending increase during a recession to shore up markets.

In both the USSR and China, military might became an important part of the communist regime.

intended, though, making it the basis of a full-blown libertarian dismantling of the authority of social structures.

In *Anarchy, State and Utopia* (1974), Nozick argued that all individuals are "self-owners", so all individual rights – over mind, body, abilities or goods – must be considered as property rights. These rights are absolute and can't be overridden by the state or any other collective authority. So a welfare state that takes money in taxes is institutionalized theft, and progressive taxation a form of forced labor. Even if the state is democratically sanctioned, it is a violation of the individual's rights to take their time, money or labor. He proposed a minimalist "nightwatchman" state that protected its citizens from violence and enforced laws governing the fair acquisition and transfer of property. Other functions often taken on by the state, including education, healthcare and welfare, were to be left to private businesses and charities.

Socio-economic development would be driven by the free market, unregulated by rent controls or minimum wage agreements, both of which violate the rights of the individual. Instead of distributive justice, Nozick preferred "entitlement justice": there would be no state assets to be distributed,

> *"He called me a sentimental idealist and he was right; I called him a vain man, perfidious and crafty, and I also was right."*
>
> Bakunin, on meeting Marx (1844)

> "Everything within the state, nothing outside the state, nothing against the state."
>
> Italian dictator Benito Mussolini (1883–1945)

and an individual would be entitled to anything justly acquired. The "justness" of acquisition was defined by a complex set of rules governing acquisition and transfers.

Some aspects of Nozick's political philosophy found favour with right-wing politicians of the 1980s – but not all. He saw the criminalization of prostitution, suicide and drug-taking as violations of the right of individuals to do whatever they liked with their bodies.

The *anti-foundationalist* Richard Rorty

(1931–2007) advocated cutting down the state's role to a minimum that simply protected people from cruelty or extreme poverty. He saw that there were, in practical terms, limits to how far anti-foundationalist politics could be implemented and hoped that with imagination and creativity people would be able to "describ[e] a future in terms which the past did not use".

Into the future

We are now living in that future in which the state did little to intervene and it's not looking good for most people.

Friedrich Nietzsche observed, over a century ago, that historically it is the strong

The need for a certain degree of personal freedom should bring an end to all oppressive regimes sooner or later. According to Chomsky, humans have an innate intolerance of oppressive regimes and these can never completely subdue the minds of their citizens – there will always be rebels.

who come to dominate in society: the self-realized, those who can control their passions and channel the "will to power" into a creative force. He said that they have a moral duty to help the weaker:

"The man of virtue, too, helps the unfortunate, but not, or almost not, out of pity, but prompted by an urge which is begotten by the excess of power."

Nietzsche, *Beyond Good and Evil* (1886)

There has been a bout of humanitarianism among American billionaires, with some of the most successful people giving away large sums of money to support the arts, medical research or education, in their own communities and elsewhere in the world. But in general, a minimalist state has not worked. The good will of a few individuals is not enough, and the gap between rich and poor is growing ever wider.

PHILOSOPHERSPEAK: LIBERTARIANISM

Libertarianism is used in different ways, but generally applies to a belief in the innate freedom of individuals and the reduction or removal of the state. Anarchism is extreme libertarianism.

ALL'S FAIR IN LOVE AND . . . BASKETBALL

Nozick illustrated the concept of entitlement justice using the example of a famous basketball player, Wilt Chamberlain.

Assume that everyone in the US starts with an equal amount of money. They can all choose to spend it as they wish. Chamberlain says he will only play basketball if each member of the audience pays 25 cents to him each time he plays. At the end of the season, a million people have paid to see him play, so he has $250,000. Chamberlain is now much richer than everyone else. But he is entitled to the money as each person paid freely, in full knowledge of the situation, and everyone who didn't kept their 25 cents. What can be the excuse for taking some of

Chamberlain's money away and redistributing it? If the first distribution was fair (when everyone was given the same money), surely the new distribution of wealth is still fair?

A silent, peaceful protest in Greece in 2012 in response to the state's introduction of extreme austerity measures. Many saw these measures as the state intervening too late and punishing the victims rather than the perpetrators of mismanagement in a global free-market economy.

Society and sociology

The French philosopher Auguste Comte (1798–1857) was the first to apply the methods of science to the study of people and societies. This was based on the "statics and dynamics" of society and led to the modern discipline of sociology.

Shaky beginnings

From statics, the science of forces in equilibrium, Comte concluded that no part of the "social consensus" can be changed without affecting the whole: economic, cultural and social conditions all have an effect on each other. From dynamics, the science of change, he decided that the development of society mirrors the development of intellectual progress; social orders have progressively moved through stages of theocracy, monarchy and anarchy and were due to establish a new social order led by science. At this point he rather lost his way. As he tried to find a place for the important role that religion and ideology play in social cohesion, he came to believe himself to be the high priest of a new religion of humanity.

Personal and public conscience

A natural successor was born a year after Comte's death. The French sociologist Émile Durkheim (1858–1917) undertook to show how all human societies are bound together and organized by moral rules. In *The Division of Labour in Society* (1893), he carried out a historical investigation, looking at how moral rules have actually operated in societies. Like Comte, he felt the need for a kind of "science of morality" to make this possible, and used scientific methodology to analyse the social structures he looked at. He found that as societies evolve from what he called a "primitive" to a "modern" state, there is a move from collective to individual conscience and moral rules. Traditional societies tend to be devoutly religious and most people in them share the same moral values, based on their shared faith. Any violation of the rules is often strongly condemned and can be punished severely. As societies evolve, the hold of these religious beliefs weakens, morality diverges and tolerance increases.

But instead of seeing this as the fragmentation of collective conscience, Durkeim saw it as just another expression of it: the collective conscience tolerates individuation. Individuation is just the process whereby individuals develop a variety of beliefs independent of any dominant moral authority. What emerges is "the cult of the individual" – a new moral code that emphasizes the right of individuals to develop in accordance with their own beliefs. As Durkheim put it:

"In the same way as the ideal of the less developed societies was to create or maintain as intense a shared life as possible, in which the individual was absorbed, our ideal is constantly to introduce greater equality in our social relations, in order to ensure the free unfolding of socially useful forces."

Durkheim, *The Division of Labour in Society* (1893)

The surprising conclusion is that individualism does not reflect an erosion of

The American philosopher John Rawls said the acquisition of the land in North America from the Native Americans failed the test of entitlement justice, so the land should be returned to them.

old moral values in society, but an expression of new moral values. These follow the division of labor. Modern societies don't keep a strict and simple economic order, but have diverse economic relations based on diverse beliefs and values. So the "cult of the individual" is a new moral code reflecting a new social and economic order.

Durkheim felt that it is wrong to see the

cult of the individual as the cult of the self-interested ego. A collection of egotistical individuals could not form a society at all, and modern society only works because there is universal recognition of others" interests and a diversity of interests. That recognition is demonstrated in the importance we place on equality and rights.

Justice as fairness

From Plato onwards, political philosophers have looked to design a political or judicial system that seems fair to them, or that they believe will evolve naturally or already has evolved naturally. But in the 20th century – at last, we might say – someone questioned

the basis on how we might choose the best system of government and laws. It is all very well for a Nietzsche or a Locke to decide what is best for everyone else, or for the proletariat to decide what is best for them and overthrow the existing order, but this only ever leads to a system that accords with the view of a particular section of society, whether that be peasants or philosophers. The American philosopher John Rawls (1921–2002) came up with a method for designing a fair society that is beautifully simple and seems foolproof.

Rawls was one of the most important political philosophers of the 20th century. His "Justice as Fairness" theory updates the

In Political Liberalism *(1993) Rawls described how political liberalism could create an "overlapping consensus" by encouraging people to focus on the "public reason" that united them, rather than the different beliefs and traditions that might divide them.*

social contract, protecting individual rights and promoting distributive justice at the same time. He starts from what he calls the "original position". This requires that people work from behind a "veil of ignorance" to decide what is fair. They have to decide their justice system and social structure without knowing what position they, as individuals, will occupy in society: whether they will be the most menial worker or a member of the ruling class. In this situation they are bound to adopt what he called a "maximin strategy" – a set of principles that is fair for everyone in order to ensure that they themselves do not suffer when they enter society later on. These are: "The principles that rational and free persons concerned to further their own interests would accept in an initial position of equality as defining the fundamentals of the terms of their association."

Rawls believed that people would come up with two Principles of Justice. The First (Liberty) Principle states that "each person is to have an equal right to the most extensive scheme of equal basic liberties compatible with a similar scheme of liberty for others". These basic liberties include freedom of speech, assembly, thought and conscience, and the right to hold personal property. They do not include the classic "freedoms from", like freedom from unemployment, exploitation or fear.

The Second (Justice) Principle is in two parts. To start with, everyone must have equality of opportunity in terms of gaining jobs or positions of power, and that entails equality of educational provision. The second part states that inequality is only acceptable if it raises the absolute level of the worst-off. No one should expect greater rewards simply because they were lucky enough to be born with greater gifts.

Rawls recognized that the two Principles could work against each other, so he made the Liberty Principle more or less absolute – it must take precedence, except in situations of low economic development.

Rawls refused an international application of the "Difference Principle", claiming that countries, unlike individuals, had no right to expect compensation for a lack of natural resources. He did not accept the argument put forward by the American political theorist Charles Beitz (born 1949) that global inequality, like domestic inequality in his own original theory, could only be justified when it served the interests of the poorest.

FIVE POLITICAL SYSTEMS

In 1971, Rawls assessed five political systems by reference to his Principles of Justice and Liberty:

► Laissez-faire capitalism
► State socialism with a command economy
► Welfare-state capitalism
► Property-owning democracy
► Market socialism.

Initially, he thought only the first two unworkable, but by 2001 his experience of the USA in the 1980s and 1990s led him to reject welfare-state capitalism, too. Only property-owning democracy or market socialism remain.

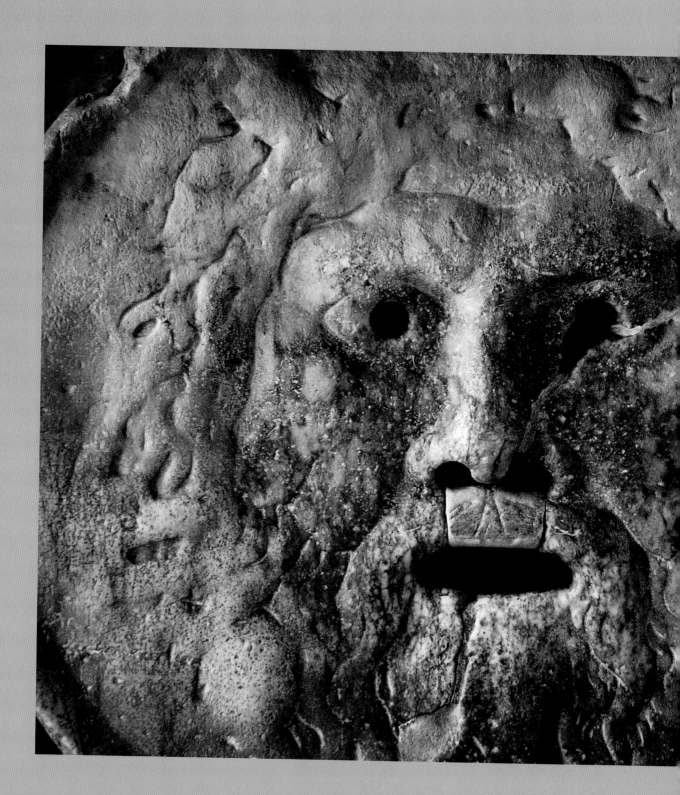

At the end of the **DAY**

"*The point of philosophy is to start with something so simple as not to seem worth stating, and to end with something so paradoxical that no one will believe it.*"

Bertrand Russell, *The Philosophy of Logical Atomism* (1918)

"*I feel that we are all philosophers, and that those who describe themselves as a philosopher simply do not have a day job to go to.*"

Kevin Warwick (quoted 2004)

The Mouth of Truth: in Renaissance Italy, citizens could post denunciations of others who had committed crimes in "mouths" dedicated to different types of crime.

Unpicking the fabric of philosophy

For the Algerian-born French post-structuralist philosopher Jacques Derrida, the meanings of words are fluid and subjective. For every individual, a word or utterance has meaning that is garnered from personal history and experience, from connotations not known by or accessible to the original speaker. The network of associations for a word extends through personal and public space and time. The lack of objective meaning has particular impact when we discuss metaphysical concepts such as "self" and "virtue". A word such as "self" necessarily implies its opposite, "other". Derrida claims that the concept of "self" is a linguistic construction with no metaphysical or ontological necessity. Of course, a philosopher dismantling language is sawing through the branch he is sitting on. He has nothing to offer in place of language and no way of justifying his authority, as he has discredited authority.

The applications of philosophy

Philosophy is a subject in which it is possible we will never agree on "right" answers. Whereas the questions in other disciplines can often be answered with empirical evidence – DNA is the means of biological inheritance, or earthquakes are caused by the movement of tectonic plates, for example – philosophy is of a different quality. The proof that reality exists, for example, will always seem to some people just silly intellectual gymnastics: they just know reality exists because they feel they are experiencing it and that's good enough. In terms of everyday life, of course, it *is* good

Accused of the murder of his girlfriend Reeva Steenkamp in 2013, Oscar Pistorius "did not want to shoot his girlfriend; he wanted to shoot an unknown intruder", according to his lawyer. Is killing the wrong person a moral defence? Does it matter which person is killed? Does that suggest one life is worth more than another?

enough. But there are many applications of philosophy that make answers to a lot of the questions important.

Personal rights and responsibilities and security of knowledge are important in jurisprudence, for example. Morals and relationships between individuals are important in law-making. Ethical questions are ever more frequently asked in science and medicine. If neurology now shows, as it well might, that what we think of as free will is not so free after all, that will have implications for how we should deal with crime. And attitudes towards God – whether we believe in one, whether He differs from the God or gods that others believe in – still cause wars and violence around the world.

Even in our day-to-day dealings with other people, engagement with philosophy can lead us to a more thoughtful and perhaps consistent position. Which rights and responsibilities do we feel we have

in our relationships with partners, parents and children? Which choices are we free to make?

For each individual, the question of how to spend our lives, which pursuits are worthwhile, is one that must be asked – we all seek Kierkegaard's "idea for which I can live and die". The answers will differ, but that doesn't matter. Ultimately, philosophy is a personal pursuit worthy of all thinking people.

Philosophy need not be some lofty and inaccessible discipline. Richard Rorty (1931–2007) believed that philosophers had developed too high an opinion of themselves and their endeavour. He disparaged the more esoteric and abstruse bits of philosophy, saying that there are no *a priori* philosophical truths to be discovered. He felt that society would do better to learn about humankind and morality from novels than from philosophers, and the traditional form of philosophy has outlived its usefulness. Of course, that didn't go down well with

By 2001, the realization that the healthcare system in the USA penalized the poor led philosopher John Rawls to reject welfare-state capitalism as unworkable.

other professional philosophers, and he was accused of abandoning philosophy, even becoming an anti-philosopher. Like Jacques Derrida, he sawed through the branch he was sitting on. But there is one useful lesson to be learned – and it is something that Bertrand Russell said first. Russell spent most of his philosophical career working on logic and mathematics, but in his later days he became more concerned with ethics and politics. Yet he denied this was the work of a philosopher. It was, perhaps, his most important philosophical work:

"On these questions I did not write in my capacity as a philosopher; I wrote as a human being who suffered from the state of the world, wished to find some way of improving it, and was anxious to speak in plain terms to others who had similar feelings."

Glossary

antithesis An opposition between two things.

aphorism a concise statement of a scientific principle.

cultural relativism The principle that an individual person's beliefs and activities should be understood by others in terms of that individual's own culture.

empiricism The theory that all knowledge is derived from sensory experience.

existentialism A theory that emphasizes the existence of the individual person as a free and responsible agent determining their own development through acts of the will.

idealism Any of various systems of thought in which the objects of knowledge are held to be in some way dependent on the activity of mind.

intentionality The quality of mental states that consists in their being directed toward some object or state of affairs.

neoplatonism is a modern term used to designate a tradition of philosophy that arose in the 3rd century AD and persisted until shortly after the closing of the Platonic Academy in Athens in AD 529 by Justinian I.

nominalism Associated particularly with William of Occam, the idea that universal ideas are just names without any corresponding reality, and that only particular objects exist.

pantheism A doctrine that regards the universe as a manifestation of God.

perspectivism The theory that knowledge of a subject is limited by the individual perspective from which it is viewed.

phenomenalism The idea that human knowledge is confined to the senses.

quantum theory A theory of matter and energy based on the concept of quanta, especially quantum mechanics.

rationalism The theory that reason rather than experience is the foundation of certainty in knowledge.

realism the attitude of accepting a situation as it is and being prepared to deal with it accordingly.

skepticism The theory that certain knowledge is impossible.

semiotics The study of signs and symbols and their interpretation.

Stoicism The school of thought that taught that virtue is based on knowledge, and that the wise live in harmony with the divine Reason that governs nature.

teleology The explanation of phenomena by the purpose they serve.

theism The belief in the existence of a god or gods.

utilitarianism The idea that actions are right if they are useful or for the benefit of a majority.

utopia A place in which everything is perfect.

For More Information

The American Philosophical Association (APA)

University of Delaware

31 Amstel Avenue, Newark, DE 19716

(302) 831-1112

Website: www.apaonline.org

The APA promotes the professional development of philosophers to foster greater understanding and appreciation of the value of philosophical study.

Canadian Philosophical Association (CPA)

PO Box 47077; rpo Blackburn Hamlet

Gloucester ON K1B 5P9

e-mail: administration@acpcpa.ca

Website: www.acpcpa.ca

The CPA promotes philosophical scholarship and education across Canada.

International Society for the History of Philosophy of Science (HOPOS)

Virginia Polytechnic Institute and State University

925 Prices Fork Road

Blacksburg, VA 24061

(540) 231-6267

Website: www.hopos.org

HOPOS is devoted to promoting research on the history of the philosophy of science.

Websites

Because of the changing nature of Internet links, Rosen Publishing has developed an online list of websites related to the subject of this book. This site is updated regularly. Please use this link to access the list:

http://www.rosenlinks.com/HHSS/phil

For Further Reading

Adamson, Peter. *A History of Philosophy without Any Gaps*. New York, NY: Oxford University Press, 2015.

Blackburn, Simon. *A Compelling Introduction to Philosophy*. New York, NY: Oxford University Press, 2001.

Buckingham, Will. *The Philosophy Book*. London, England: DK Publishing, 2011.

Klein, Daniel M. *Every Time I Find the Meaning of Life, They Change It: Wisdom of the Great Philosophers on How to Live*. New York, NY: Penguin, 2015.

Kleinman, Paul. *Philosophy 101: From Plato and Socrates to Ethics and Metaphysics, an Essential Primer on the History of Thought*. Blue Ash, OH: Adams Media, 2013.

Pagden, Dr Anthony. *The Enlightenment*. New York, NY: Random House, 2013.

Scott, A. O. *Better Living through Criticism: How to Think about Art, Pleasure, Beauty, and Truth*. New York, NY: Penguin Press, 2016.

Stokes, Philip. *Philosophy: 100 Essential Thinkers: The Ideas That Have Shaped Our World*. London, England: Arcturus, 2012.

Warburton, Nigel. *A Little History of Philosophy*. New Haven, CT: Yale University Press, 2011.

Warburton, Nigel. *Philosophy: The Classics*. London, England: Routledge, 2014.

Weeks, Marcus. *Heads up Philosophy*. London, England: DK Publishing, 2014.

Index